Speak Spanish Now for
Public Safety Officials

Speak Spanish Now for Public Safety Officials

A Customized Learning Approach for Law Enforcement and Department of Corrections Staff

Brian K. Jones

CAROLINA ACADEMIC PRESS

Durham, North Carolina

Library of Congress Cataloging-in-Publication Data

Jones, Brian K. (Brian Keith), 1971-

Speak Spanish now for public safety officials : a customized learning approach for law enforcement and department of corrections staff / Brian K. Jones.

p. cm.

Includes bibliographical references.

ISBN 978-1-59460-433-1 (alk. paper)

1. Spanish language--Conversation and phrase books (for police) 2. Law enforcement--Terminology. 3. Spanish language--Glossaries, vocabularies, etc. I. Title.

PC4120.P64J66 2008

468.2'421--dc22   2008037103

CAROLINA ACADEMIC PRESS
700 Kent Street
Durham, North Carolina
Tel: (919) 489-7486
Fax: (919) 493-5668
www.cap-press.com

Printed in the United States of America.

This book is dedicated to my family for all of their love and support.

Contents

Preface

A Customized Learning Approach to Language

The purpose of this text is to assist those in the public safety sector with effective, immediate communication with Spanish-speaking persons. Therefore, this book's approach is to teach straightforward, oral communication that requires the learner to verbally produce while relying little on listening skills. It is intended primarily as one-way communication and does not require the learning of grammar or the development of written communique. However, certain anticipated responses have been included for you. Even if the speaker does not use the exact answer, you will be able to recognize fragments and then take control of the conversation. Upon successfully mastering the phrases of the text, the learner will be able to manage situations they commonly encounter on a daily basis, give instructions and commands, ascertain personal information and interact with Spanish-speaking persons in a culturally appropriate manner.

Using this text

This text has been designed to promote communication in Spanish for professionals in the field of public safety, with primary focus on law enforcement officials and department of corrections staff. However, professionals in closely related fields, such as security, court officers and social workers, may find this text practical. Since not all sections of the text may be specific to each group's job duties, the text allows you to pick and choose what you will learn and concentrate on those areas that are most beneficial to you and your respective profession. The pages have been perforated so you can easily remove sections you will not use in order to customize the book or make the most used pages more portable.

In learning the words and phrases in this text, you will be concentrating on oral communication. You will only write in Spanish when preparing note cards or preparing phrases to be used during an activity unless it is a requirement of your curriculum. Grammatical explanations are not necessary for any of the information you will be learning. Your instructor will lead you through a wide variety of communicative exercises that will help you internalize these phrases and their meanings and get away from the daunting task of rote memorization. The accompanying CD will enable you to listen to the phrases and practice their pronunciation. Your instructor may also choose to provide you with strategies that will make the CD more beneficial to you as a study aid. The CD may be used in class but is also highly recommended as an independent study aid.

The sections have been designated titles to help you manage the selection of the material you will choose to learn. However, make sure to glance through all of them for miscellaneous phrases you may find beneficial in your interactions with Spanish-speaking persons. Feel free to mix and match phrases from various sections in order to tailor the information you will need to convey to and/or obtain from the other person. Most of the time, the phrases follow a logical order for their delivery. However, there is no prescribed order that must be followed each time they are used.

Immediately before each set of phrases, when appropriate, you will find a section titled BEFORE YOU BEGIN. These sections present pertinent information that will enable public safety officials to better understand the cultural differences between Hispanic and non-Hispanic persons and thus manage a situation more effectively. Current statistics and important relevant information that focus on the Hispanic population have been included.

Finally, at the end of most chapters, you will find a **NOTES** section followed by a **PRACTICAL ACTIVITIES** section that includes activities that concentrate on the respective chapter and its content. Where applicable, an optional **CYBER-INVESTIGATION** exercise (Internet search activity) meant to build upon cultural information presented in the **BEFORE YOU BEGIN** section has been included.

Pronunciation

The purpose of the pronunciation patterns found directly above each Spanish phrase is to immediately generate proper or nearly proper pronunciation. By following these easy guidelines, communication becomes instantaneous. The words and sounds used in the pronunciation patterns are based on those used in English, so say what you see. Practice exercises to aid you in interpreting the pronunciation patterns and to prepare you for making those sounds correctly follow these brief explanations. Be sure to follow them in the designated order.

Instructions for reading the pronunciation patterns:

1. The separation of words has been indicated by one or more spaces.

    Example: *boo^ay-nohs dee-ahs.* (two word phrase)
    Buenos días.

2. The separation of syllables has been indicated by a hyphen.

    Example: *boo^ay-nohs dee-ahs.* (each word has two syllables)
    Buenos días.

3. Syllables written in bolded letters are emphasized when spoken.

    Example: *boo^ay-nohs dee-ahs.* (emphasis on **boo^ay** and **dee**)
    Buenos días.

4. Syllables written in letters not bolded are not emphasized.

    Example: *boo^ay-nohs dee-ahs.* (no emphasis on -nohs and -ahs)
    Buenos días.

5. The upward pointing arrow, or the (^) sign, indicates a combination of sounds to be pronounced as one (1) syllable (one sound).

    Example: *boo^ay-nohs dee-ahs.* (**boo^ay** is one sound)
    Buenos días.

6. The double r you will see indicates a rolled or trilled "r" sound.

    Example: *rray-goo-lahr.* (rr of *rray* is rolled/trilled)
    Regular.

The double *r*, or "*rr*" in Spanish, is represented by "*rr*" in the pronunciation key. Do the best you can to imitate the sound but do not get frustrated, as long as you are making the effort you will be understood. Keep practicing and it will come with time. Likewise, anyone who has any prior knowledge of Spanish pronunciation may know that the Spanish *v* is often pronounced as a soft English *b*, although some dialects of spoken Spanish do pronounce the Spanish *v* the same as the English *v*. However, for the sake of consistency and simplicity, the Spanish v has been represented as the letter b in the pronunciation patterns throughout the text and may be pronounced as such.

Introduction Exercise:

With a partner or as a group, randomly select phrases from the text, analyze them and identify each of the above elements from the pronunciation patterns explanations. Do not practice pronunciation yet. Just become familiar with how to interpret the pronunciation patterns. You must practice the following pronunciation exercises thoroughly before attempting to read the pronunciation patterns for the phrases!

Lingual Aerobics (so to speak) . . .

Getting started: Just like any other muscle in your body that is not accustomed to certain motions and actions, the tongue and mouth are no different. These exercises will help you warm up these muscles and form the correct positions with your mouth and tongue to produce relatively authentic Spanish pronunciation from the very beginning.

Pronunciation Exercise 1

This oral exercise is to help you become used to the basic sounds you will use and see throughout this text, all of which are based on the five basic vowel sounds of the Spanish alphabet – A, E, I, O, U. Though they are the same five vowels found in English, their sounds are rather different. In order to facilitate their production, in practicing this exercise, say exactly what you see as you would in English. Start by saying the words and sounds, going column by column (in sequence according to numbers) together as a group, then row by row, individually, in small groups, then in pairs, etc. Remember, the sounds bolded in the first column should be applied to the combinations you will practice in each column that follows. These bolded sounds are the actual sounds of the corresponding Spanish vowel.

Spanish Vowel	#1	#2	#3	#4	#5	#6	#7	#8	#9
A	ha**h**	**ah**	bah	kah	lah	mah	sah	tah	yah
E	d**ay**	**ay**	bay	kay	lay	may	say	tay	yay
I	s**ee**	**ee**	bee	kee	lee	mee	see	tee	yee
O	**oh**	**oh**	boh	koh	loh	moh	soh	toh	yoh
U	f**ood**	**oo**	boo	koo	loo	moo	soo	too	yoo

Pronunciation Exercise 2

The second practice exercise builds upon the previous one by introducing you to sound combinations you will use and see throughout the text. Practice these in the same manner as the first set. Remember to make letters linked with the upward pointing arrow (^) one syllable (one sound).

#1	#2	#3	#4	#5	#6
stah	boo^ay	tree	ahr	nahs	tahr
chah	stay	skree	ayr	nays	tayr
grah	poo^ay	moo^ee	eer	nees	teer
blah	tray	ghee*	ohr	nohs	tohr
trah	goo^ay	flee	oor	noos	toor

* This *g* is like the *g* sound in the word *get* but pronounced with the *long ee* sound.

Pronunciation Exercise 3

Starting with column 1, make sure to emphasize the bolded letters according to the pronunciation key. Once again, remember to make letters linked with the upward pointing arrow (^) one syllable (one sound).

#1	#2	#3	#4
gah-nahs	ah-**sayr**	**tee^ay**-nay	nah-see-**mee^ayn**-toh
dohn-day	ay-spah-**nyohl**	**kee^ay**-rayn	sah-rahm-**pee^ohn**
pah-gahn	rray-spee-**rahr**	kee-**see^ay**-rah	dee^ah-**bay**-tays
ah-nyoh**	door-**meer**	ee-**stoh**-ree^ah	ee-payr-tayn-**see^ohn**
kwahn-toh	rray-say-**tahr**	**see^ayn**-toh	see-**ghee^ayn**-tay

 * This *g* is like the *g sound* in the word *get* but pronounced with the *long ee* sound.
** The *ny* is pronounced like the *ni* in the English word *onion*.

Pronunciation Exercise 4

Look through the text paying attention only to the pronunciation key and practice random examples as a class then in pairs.

Speak Spanish Now
for
Public Safety Officials

Chapter 1

Getting Started: Greetings, Courtesy Expressions, and Goodbyes

Before You Begin

The Hispanic culture is a very respectful one full of customs and traditions. Regardless of a person's socioeconomic rank, the expectation of mutual respect still exists. Spanish speakers lean toward formality, even in their treatment of one another. Using phrases and expressions that are characteristic of familiar relationships - such as using the first name of a person instead of the appropriate title and last name for a person you have just met - may be considered rude or as poor manners. The words and phrases you learn throughout this text, unless otherwise noted, exemplify the etiquette practiced by Hispanics. They are all appropriate for the environment in which you will use them and the interactions you will have with Spanish-speakers. Remember that being courteous is the key to establishing trust with Hispanics.

Phrases

English	Pronunciation & Spanish
1. Hello.	*oh*-lah. Hola.
2. Good morning.	*boo^ay*-nohs *dee*-ahs. Buenos días.[1]
3. Good afternoon.	*boo^ay*-nahs *tahr*-days. Buenas tardes.[1]
4. Good evening. / Good night.	*boo^ay*-nahs *noh*-chays. Buenas noches. [1]
5. Sir / Mr.	sayn-*yohr*. Señor.
6. Ma'am / Mrs.	sayn-*yoh*-rah. Señora.[2]
7. Miss / Ms.	sayn-yoh-*ree*-tah. Señorita. [2]
8. How are you (today)?	*koh*-moh ay-*stah* (oh^ee)? ¿Cómo está (hoy)?
9. (Very) well/fine. (And you?)	(moo^ee) bee^ayn (ee oo-*stayd*?) (Muy) bien. (¿Y Ud.?)[3]

10. Okay.	*rray-goo-**lahr**.* Regular.	
11. So, so.	*ah-**see** ah-**see**.* Así, así.	
12. Not (very) well.	*(moo^ee) mahl.* (Muy) mal.[4]	
13. More or less.	*mahs oh **may**-nohs.* Más o menos.	
14. I'm sorry.	*loh **see^ayn**-toh.* Lo siento.	
15. Until later.	***ah**-stah **loo^ay**-goh.* Hasta luego.	
16. Goodbye.	*ah-**dee^ohs**.* Adiós.	
17. Thank you (very much).	*(moo-chahs) **grah**-see^ahs.* (Muchas) gracias.	
18. Please.	*pohr fah-**bohr**.* Por favor.	
19. You're welcome.	*day **nah**-dah.* De nada.	
20. Pardon. [stating excuse me **after** an action]	*payr-**dohn**.* Perdón.	
21. Excuse me. [to get someone's attention]	*dee-**skool**-pay.* Disculpe.	
22. Excuse me. [stating excuse me **before** an action]	*kohn payr-**mee**-soh.* Con permiso.	
23. Okay / Fine.	*ay-**stah** bee^ayn.* Está bien.[5]	
24. Have a nice day.	*kay **pah**-say oon boo^ayn **dee**-ah.* Qué pase un buen día.	
25. At your service.	*ah soos **ohr**-day-nays.* A sus órdenes.[6]	
26. A pleasure (to see you).	***moo**-choh **goo**-stoh (**bayr**-loh/lah).* Mucho gusto (verlo/la). [7]	
27. Yes / No. Of course.	*see / noh **koh**-moh noh / pohr soo-**poo^ay**-stoh.* Sí / no. Como no / Por supuesto.	

Notes

[1] For simplicity's sake, use *Buenos días* from early morning (generally sun-up) to noon, *Buenas tardes* from noon to sun-down and *Buenas noches* from sun-down to early morning. *Buenas noches* may be used as a greeting or a goodbye after sundown as well.

[2] Though a woman may not appear young, if she is not married, she is still a *señorita*. Also, *señorita* is often abbreviated as *Srta.*, *señora* as *Sra.* and *señor* as *Sr.*

[3] The word *usted* is commonly abbreviated as *Ud.* Whenever you see this abbreviation, make sure to say the entire word.

[4] This phrase is a question of wellbeing and not one of a diagnostic nature, the literal translation of *muy mal* (very badly) is implied.

[5] This is very common for expressing agreement and comprehension. Another possible translation would be the English *alright*.

[6] Also expressed by the phrase *Para servirle* (**pah**-rah sayr-**beer**-lay) or *Estoy a su servicio* (ay-**stoh**^*ee* ah soo sayr-**bee**-see^oh).

[7] If speaking to a *male*, use *verlo*; if speaking to a *female* use *verla*.

Practical Activities

A) Meet and Greet

Instructions: Based on the following information, orally compose mini-conversations in which you *meet and greet* the persons indicated in an appropriate manner. Remember, speak ONLY in Spanish.

You say/ask . . .	The person says/responds/asks . . .

mini-conversation I

1. Good morning to an unmarried female.	Hello.
2. How are you doing?	Not very well.
3. I'm sorry.	Thank you.
4. Until later.	Goodbye.

mini-conversation II

1. Good afternoon to a married male.	Good afternoon.
2. How are you doing?	Very well, thank you. And you?
3. So-so.	It's nice to see you.
4. Thank you.	Have a nice day.

mini-conversation III

1. Good evening to a married female.	Hello. How are you today?
2. Very well. And you?	Fine.
3. At your service.	Thank you very much.

B) Appropriate Responses

Instructions: Based on each scenario described below, select the Spanish phrase(s) from this section that would be most appropriate and explain why.

1. You need to get someone's attention. _____

_____

2. You need to leave a conversation to answer the phone. _____

_____

3. Someone says he/she does not feel well today. _____

_____

4. You see someone you've not seen in some time. _____

_____

5. Someone asks how you are doing today. _____

_____

6. You are saying goodbye to a female in the evening. _____

_____

C) When and where?

Instructions: Take a few moments and think to yourself, when and where you would use the expressions and phrases presented in this section in your respective position. Then take turns sharing this information in pairs, groups or as a class. You may even want to discuss why you would not need certain phrases, as well.

Identifying Yourself and Preliminary Scene Assessments

Before You Begin

Fear of police and deportation make Hispanics easy targets, not only for criminals but for law enforcement as well. This fear results in many Hispanics not reporting crimes or calling for emergency assistance. On the other hand, while most Hispanics may fear public safety officials, they also respect them. However, their view of law enforcement is often tainted by preconceived notions instilled in them by the corrupt legal systems of their home countries. Many Latin American countries have extremely corrupt legal systems due to economic uncertainty, social problems and poor education. Surprisingly, some countries have no one single entity that makes unbiased, impartial decisions based on law. These factors translate into an ineffective legal system where the majority of crimes go unpunished and the power of authority is controlled by an elite few.

Since a Hispanic's nonverbal communication is strongly influenced by respect, direct eye contact may be avoided between Hispanics and authority figures, such as police officers, correctional officers, etc. due to a perceived class distinction. This should not be misconstrued as disrespect or indicative of lying since this is a cultural norm in the Hispanic community.

Phrases

English	Pronunciation & Spanish
1. I'm . . .	*soh^ee* Soy . . . [1]
Mr. —.	*ayl sayn-**yohr** —.* el señor —[1]
Mrs. —.	*lah sayn-**yoh**-rah —.* la señora —.
Ms. —.	*lah sayn-yoh-**ree**-tah —.* la señorita —.
Officer —.	*ayl/lah ah-**hayn**-tay day poh-lee-**see**-ah —.* el/la agente de policía —.
Sergeant —.	*ayl/lah sahr-**hayn**-toh/tah —.* el/la sargento/a —.
Lieutenant —.	*ayl tay-**nee^ayn**-tay / lah tay-**nee^ayn**-tah —.* el teniente / la tenienta —.
Captain —.	*ayl kah-pee-**tahn** / lah kah-pee-**tah**-nah —.* el capitán / la capitana —.
Agent —.	*ayl/lah ah-**hayn**-tay —.* el/la agente —.
Police Inspector —.	*ayl een-spayk-**tohr**/lah een-spayk-**toh**-rah day poh-lee-**see**-ah —.* el inspector / la inspectora de policía —.
Corrections Officer —.	*ayl/lah ah-**hayn**-tay day koh-rrayk-**see^oh**-nays —.* el/la agente de correcciones —.

Bailiff/Sheriff —.	*ayl/lah ahl-goo^ah-**seel** —.* el/la alguacil —.²
Detective —.	*ayl/lah day-tayk-**tee**-bay —.* el/la detective —.
Chief —.	*ayl **hay**-fay/lah **hay**-fah —.* el jefe / la jefa —.
Deputy —.	*ayl/lah dee-poo-**tah**-doh/dah —.* el/la diputado/a —.
Patrolman —.	*ayl/lah pah-troo-**yay**-roh/rah —.* el/la patrullero/a —.
Warden —.	*ayl/lah goo^ahr-**dee^ahn**/lah goo^ahr-**dee^ah**-nah (day lah pree-**see^ohn**) —* el guardián / la guardiana (de la prisión) —.
Counselor —.	*ayl/lah kohn-say-**hay**-roh/rah —.* el/la consejero/a —.
Dispatcher —.	*ayl/lah day-spah-chah-**dohr**(-ah) —.* el/la despachador/a —.

2. I'm here to help (you).	*ay-**stoh^ee** ah-**kee** pah-rah ah^ee-yoo-**dahr**(-lay).* Estoy aquí para ayudar(le).
3. I'm going to help (you).	*boh^ee ah ah^ee-yoo-**dahr**-(lay).* Voy a ayudar(le).
4. Do you speak English?	*__ah__-blah een-**glays**?* ¿Habla inglés?
5. Does someone here speak English?	*ah^ee **ahl**-ghee^ayn ah-**kee** kay **ah**-blay een-**glays**?* ¿Hay alguien aquí que hable inglés?
6. Yes.	*see.* Sí.
7. No.	*noh.* No.
8. A little.	*oon **poh**-koh.* Un poco.
9. I don't speak Spanish.	*noh **ah**-bloh ay-spahn-**yohl**.* No hablo español.
10. I speak very little Spanish.	*__ah__-bloh moo^ee **poh**-koh ay-spahn-**yohl**.* Hablo muy poco español.
11. Excuse me.	*dee-**skool**-pay.* Disculpe. [to get someone's attention]
12. Wait (right) here.	*ay-**spay**-ray(n) ah-**kee** (**mees**-moh).* Espere(n) aquí (mismo).³

13. I'll be right back.

*yah **boo**^ayl-boh.*
Ya vuelvo.

14. Just a moment, please.

*oon moh-**mayn**-toh pohr fah-**bohr**.*
Un momento, por favor.

15. Who needs immediate assistance?

*kee^ayn nay-say-**see**-tah day ah^ee-**yoo**-dah een-may-**dee**^**ah**-tah?.*
¿Quién necesita de ayuda inmediata?

16. Is anyone sick or injured?

***ahl**-ghee^ayn ay-**stah** ayn-**fayr**-moh oh lay-see^oh-**nah**-doh?*
¿Alguien está enfermo o lesionado?

17. You stay where you are, (please).

***kay**-day-say **dohn**-day ay-**stay** (pohr fah-**bohr**).*
Quédese donde esté, (por favor).

18. Everyone stay where you are, please.

***kay**-dayn-say **dohn**-day ay-**stayn** (pohr fah-**bohr**).*
Quédense donde estén, (por favor).

19. Come here, (please).

***bayn**-gah(n) ah-**kee** (pohr fah-**bohr**).*
Venga(n) aquí, (por favor). ³

20. Calm down.

***kahl**-may(n)-say.*
Cálme(n)se. ³

21. Sit down (now).

***see**^**ayn**-tay(n)-say (ah-**oh**-rah).*
Siénte(n)se (ahora). ³

22. Wait for further instructions.

*ay-**spay**-ray(n) een-strook-**see**^**oh**-nays ah-dee-see^oh-**nah**-lays.*
Espere(n) instrucciones adicionales. ³

23. You be quiet and don't move.

***kah**-yay-say ee noh say **moo**^**ay**-bah.*
Cállese y no se mueva.

24. Everyone be quiet and don't move.

***kah**-yayn-say ee noh say **moo**^**ay**-bahn.*
Cállense y no se muevan.

25. I don't understand.

*noh kohm-**prayn**-doh.*
No comprendo.

Please repeat it (slower).

*pohr fah-**bohr**, rray-**pee**-tah-loh (mahs day-**spah**-see^oh).*
Por favor, repítalo (más despacio).

26. Thank you for your patience.

*lay ah-grah-**days**-koh lah pah-**see**^**ayn**-see^ah.*
Le agradezco la paciencia.

27. Do you need . . .

*nay-say-**see**-tah . . .*
¿Necesita . . .

an ambulance?

*oo-nah ahm-boo-**lahn**-see^ah?*
una ambulancia?

the fire department?

*ah lohs bohm-**bay**-rohs?*
a los bomberos?

the paramedics?

*ah lohs pah-rah-**may**-dee-kohs?*
a los paramédicos?

Notes

[1] Where given as options, use *el* (and the *-o ending* of the title if noted) for a *male*. Use *la* (and the *-a ending* of the title if noted) for a *female*.

[2] Other possible terms you may hear are *chérif* (**chay-reef**) or *shérif* (**shay-reef**). Of course, these are more anglicized terms since there is not an exact cultural equivalent.

[3] The *"(n)"* in the commands given in this chapter indicates the possibility of a *singular form* and a *plural form*. For example, the command *"Come,"* as in *"Come with me,"* appears as *"Venga(n)."* To tell one person *"Come,"* use *"Venga."* If addressing two or more people use *"Vengan."*

Practical Activities
Identifying Yourself and Preliminary Scene Assessments

A) Who am I?

Instructions: From the titles provided in this section, write below which one applies to you. Make sure to use the correct form depending upon your gender. If your title is not listed and your instructor is not sure (since this information can be very specific depending on your job duties), simply use the appropriate title for Mr., Mrs. or Ms.

Then, using the phrase from this chapter *I'm here to help*, tell your nearest two neighbors who you are and that you are *here to help*. Try to do this as much as possible without looking at the Spanish text.

"*Soy* _____."

B) Situations

Instructions: For each situation given, select the appropriate phrases/expressions from this section that would best convey the information indicated.

1. You arrive at the scene of an emergency and state who you are, that you are here to help and ask if anyone needs immediate assistance.

2. You state that you don't speak much Spanish and ask if someone speaks English. A person says "a little" to which you respond "come here, please." You then tell everyone else to calm down and wait for further instructions.

3. You need to gain control over a group of inmates/detainees. Tell them to stay where they are, be quiet and don't move.

4. After arriving at the scene of an accident you ask the victims if anyone is sick or injured. A young man begins to mutter incoherently. You go over to him and state that you speak a little Spanish and ask him to repeat what he said. You realize he is not well and ask if he needs an ambulance.

C) Phrase fragments

Instructions: Complete each phrase fragment given by either saying the entire phrase aloud or writing the missing information. After you have completed them all, practice saying each one aloud in pairs, as a group or as a class and give the English meaning.

1. Le agradezco _____.

2. Un momento _____.

3. ¿ _____ que hable español?

4. ¿ _____ los paramédicos?

5. Cállese y no _____.

6. _____ aquí mismo.

7. ¿Necesita una _____?

8. Hablo muy _____.

Cyber-Investigation

In **Before You Begin** you read about the reluctance of many Hispanics to report crime and learned a few of the reasons why. What is being done in the U. S. to change the perception of Public Safety Officials by Hispanics? What are some of your suggestions?

Chapter 2

Multipurpose Interview for Personal Data and Information

Before You Begin

Hispanics will have varying degrees of language skills, both in Spanish and English. Depending upon their level of education, they may be literate, semi-literate or illiterate in their native language. Also, Spanish may not be their first language either, but rather an indigenous Latin American language. Likewise, depending upon the length of time they have spent in the United States, their knowledge of the English language and culture will vary greatly. Since a deep sense of pride is innate to the Hispanic culture, it may be difficult to immediately recognize the abilities of the person with whom you are dealing. However, assess the situation as your interaction progresses with care and respect and be sure to avoid causing him or her any sense of shame or embarrassment.

Unlike many Americans who have a first, middle and last name, the majority of Hispanics have a first name (or more) followed by two surnames. These surnames consist first of the father's surname followed by the mother's maiden name. It is important to understand how to distinguish these components of a Hispanic name for the sake of alphabetizing documents, etc. Hispanic names are ordered according to the father's surname unless the person has a preference.

For example:

If *Sara **Montero*** and *Pedro **García*** have a child named *Miguel*, the child's complete name would be *Miguel García Montero*. His last name is technically *García* and would appear as such on documents. Likewise, he would be alphabetized under the letter *G* for *García.*

Phrases

English	Pronunciation & Spanish
1. I'm . . .	*soo^ee . . .* Soy . . . [1]
2. I need to ask you some questions.	*lay nay-say-**see**-toh ah-**sayr** oo-nahs pray-**goon**-tahs.* Le necesito hacer unas preguntas.
3. It's important that you answer them	*ays eem-pohr-**tahn**-tay **see^aym**-pray kohn-tay-**stahr*** Es importante siempre contestar
truthfully.	*kohn lah bayr-**dahd.*** con la verdad.

4. What is your . . .

koo^ahl ays soo . . .
¿Cuál es su . . .

full name?

*nohm-bray kohm-**play**-toh?*
nombre completo?

father's last name?

*ah-pay-**yee**-doh pah-tayr-**nahl**?*
apellido paternal?

mother's maiden name?

*ah-pay-**yee**-doh mah-tayr-**nahl**?*
apellido maternal?

5. My name is (+ name).

*may **yah**-moh . . .*
Me llamo . . .

6. My name is (+ name).

*mee **nohm**-bray ays . . .*
Mi nombre es . . .

7. Do you have a nickname?

***tee^ay**-nay ahl-**goon** ah-**poh**-doh?*
¿Tiene algún apodo?

8. Will you write the information for me

*may ay-**skree**-bay lah een-fohr-mah-**see^ohn***
¿Me escribe la información

here?

*ah-**kee**?*
aquí?

9. Can you read and write?

***poo^ay**-day lay-**ayr** ee ay-skree-**beer**?*
¿Puede leer y escribir?

10. What is your level of education?

*koo^ahl ays soo nee-**bayl** day ay-doo-kah-**see^ohn**?*
¿Cuál es su nivel de educación?

11. Is Spanish your first language?

*ays ay-spahn-**yohl** soo pree-**mayr** ee-**dee^oh**-mah?*
¿Es español su primer idioma?

12. Can you speak English at all?

***poo^ay**-day ah-**blahr** oon **poh**-koh day een-**glays**?*
¿Puede hablar un poco de inglés?

13. Do you understand English at all?

*kohm-**prayn**-day ayl een-**glays** oon **poh**-koh?*
¿Comprende el inglés un poco?

14. Do you need an interpreter?

*nay-say-**see**-tah ah oon een-**tayr**-pray-tay?*
¿Necesita a un intérprete?

15. How old are you?

***koo^ahn**-tohs **ahn**-yohs **tee^ay**-nay?*
¿Cuántos años tiene?

16. What is your date of birth?

*koo^ahl ays soo **fay**-chah day nah-see-**mee^ayn**-toh?*
¿Cuál es su fecha de nacimiento?

17. Where were you born?

***dohn**-day nah-**see^oh**?*
¿Dónde nació?

Town?

***poo^ay**-bloh?*
¿Pueblo?

City?

*see^oo-**dahd**?*
¿Ciudad?

State?	*ay-**stah**-doh?* ¿Estado?
18. What is your marital status?	*koo^ahl ays soo ay-**stah**-doh see-**beel**?* ¿Cuál es su estado civil?
19. Married.	*kah-**sah**-doh/dah.* Casado/a. [2]
Divorced.	*dee-bohr-**see^ah**-doh/dah.* Divorciado/a. [2]
Separated.	*say-pah-**rah**-doh/dah.* Separado/a. [2]
Single.	*sohl-**tay**-roh/rah.* Soltero/a. [2]
Widowed.	***bee^oo**-doh/dah.* Viudo/a. [2]
20. What is your address?	*koo^ahl ays soo dee-rayk-**see^ohn**?* ¿Cuál es su dirección?
21. What was your previous address?	*koo^ahl foo^ay soo dee-rayk-**see^ohn** ahn-tay-**ree^ohr**?* ¿Cuál fue su dirección anterior?
22. What is your telephone number?	*koo^ahl ays soo **noo**-may-roh day tay-**lay**-foh-noh?* ¿Cuál es su número de teléfono?
23. How tall are you?	***koo^ahn**-toh **mee**-day?* ¿Cuánto mide? [3]
24. How much do you weigh?	***koo^ahn**-toh **pay**-sah?* ¿Cuánto pesa? [3]
25. What is your religion?	*koo^ahl ays soo rray-lee-**hee^ohn**?* ¿Cuál es su religión? [4]
26. What is your nationality?	*koo^ahl ays soo nah-see^oh-nah-lee-**dahd**?* ¿Cuál es su nacionalidad? [5]
27. Are you a member of a gang?	*ays pahn-dee-**yay**-roh/rah?* ¿Es pandillero/a? [2]
28. Are you part of any club or organization?	***fohr**-mah **pahr**-tay day koo^ahl-**kee^ayr** kloob oo* ¿Forma parte de cualquier club u *ohr-gah-nee-sah-**see^ohn**?* organización?
29. Which one?	*koo^ahl?* ¿Cuál?
30. Are you here legally? [6]	*ay-**stah** ah-**kee** lay-gahl-**mayn**-tay?* ¿Está aquí legalmente?

31. Are you · · · [6]

ays . . .
¿Es . . .

    a legal resident?

*rray-see-**dayn**-tay lay-**gahl**?*
residente legal?

    a U.S citizen?

*see^oo-dah-**dah**-noh/nah ay-stah-doh-oo-nee-**dayn**-say?*
ciudadano/a estadounidense?

32. I need to see proof of your

*nay-say-**see**-toh bayr **proo^ay**-bah day soo*
Necesito ver prueba de su

    immigration status. [6]

*kohn-dee-**see^ohn** mee-grah-**toh**-ree^ah.*
condición migratoria.

33. I need to see some (photo) identification.

*nay-say-**see**-toh bayr soo ee-dayn-tee-fee-kah-**see^ohn** (kohn **foh**-toh).*
Necesito ver su identificación (con foto).

34. Do you have . . .

***tee^ay**-nay . . .*
¿Tiene . . .

    a driver's license?

*lee-**sayn**-see^ah **pah**-rah kohn-doo-**seer**?*
licencia para conducir? [7]

    an immigration number? [6]

***noo**-may-roh day een-mee-grah-**see^ohn**?*
número de inmigración?

    a social security card?

*tahr-**hay**-tah day say-**goo**-roh soh-**see^ahl**?*
tarjeta de seguro social?

    a visa?

***bee**-sah (bee-**sah**-doh)?*
visa (visado)? [8]

    a passport?

*pah-sah-**pohr**-tay?*
pasaporte?

35. Do you work?

*trah-**bah**-hah?*
¿Trabaja?

36. Where do you work?

***dohn**-day trah-**bah**-hah?*
¿Dónde trabaja?

37. What is your profession?

*koo^ahl ays soo proh-fay-**see^ohn**?*
¿Cuál es su profesión?

38. Have you ever been arrested?

*ah **see**-doh ah-rray-**stah**-doh/dah?*
¿Ha sido arrestado/a? [2]

39. Have you ever been incarcerated?

*ah **see**-doh ayn-kahr-say-**lah**-doh/dah?*
¿Ha sido encarcelado/a? [2]

40. Have you been drinking (taking drugs)?

*ah ay-**stah**-doh toh-**mahn**-doh (**droh**-gahs)?*
¿Ha estado tomando (drogas)?

41. Do you have a criminal history?

***tee^ay**-nay ahn-tay-say-**dayn**-tays kree-mee-**nah**-lays?*
¿Tiene antecedentes criminales?

42. Do you have medical problems?

***tee^ay**-nay proh-**blay**-mahs **may**-dee-kohs?*
¿Tiene problemas médicos?

	*toh-mah ahk-too^ahl-**mayn**-tay ahl-**goo**-nah may-dee-**see**-nah?*
43. Are you currently taking any medication?	¿Toma actualmente alguna medicina?

	*koh-moh say **yah**-mah lah may-dee-**see**-nah?*
44. What's the medication called?	¿Cómo se llama la medicina?

	*ay-**stah** . . .*
45. You are . . .	Está . . .
	*lee-bray **pah**-rah **eer**-say.*
free to go.	libre para irse.
	*ayn **noo^ay**-strohs ahr-**chee**-bohs.*
now on file.	en nuestros archivos.
	*ayn **noo^ay**-strah **bah**-say day **dah**-tohs.*
on our database.	en nuestra base de datos.

	*ay-**stah see^ayn**-doh day-tay-**nee**-doh/dah.*
46. You are being detained.	Está siendo detenido/a. [2]

	*kee-**see^ay**-rah ah-**sayr** oo-nah yah-**mah**-dah tay-lay-**foh**-nee-kah?*
47. Would you like to make a phone call?	¿Quisiera hacer una llamada telefónica?

	*(Noh) **poo^ay**-day ah-**sayr** . . .*
48. You can(not) make . . .	(No) puede hacer
	*oo-nah yah-**mah**-dah loh-**kahl**.*
a local call.	una llamada local.
	*oo-nah yah-**mah**-dah day **lahr**-gah dee-**stahn**-see^ah.*
a long distance call.	una llamada de larga distancia.

Notes

[1] Use the proper title from *Chapter 1 - Getting Started: Identifying Yourself and Preliminary Scene Assessments.*

[2] Use the *-o (-oh)*ending for a *male* and the *-a (-ah)* ending for a *female*.

[3] Most Latin American countries use metrics and you may have to convert your answers. See the *Appendix* for a quick access conversion chart.

[4] See the *Appendix* for a listing of religions with their pronunciation in Spanish.

[5] See the *Appendix* for a listing of nationalities with their pronunciation in Spanish.

[6] Make sure you are legally allowed to ask these questions. They are only permitted to be asked by certain government agencies and business personnel.

[7] The verb *manejar (mah-nay-hahr)* which means *to manage; to drive* is often interchangeable with *conducir*. Therefore, you may also hear *licencia de manejar* for *driver's license.*

[8] Both of these terms are commonly used for this immigration document.

Practical Activities

A) ¿Hombre o mujer? (Man or woman?)

Instructions: Review the explanation given in number 2 of the **Notes** for this section. Then, ask the question or make the statement below to a male and then a female making the necessary changes. Take turns doing this in pairs, groups or as a class and make sure to pay close attention to how the sounds are different depending upon whether a *male* or *female* is being addressed.

1. You are being detained. (male) / (female)
2. Are you a U. S. citizen? (male) / (female)
3. Are you a member of a gang? (male) / (female)
4. Are you divorced or separated? (male) / (female)
5. Have you ever been incarcerated? (male) / (female)

B) Obtaining Personal Information

Part I - Instructions: First, write the numbers one through ten in a column on a piece of paper. Then, choose 10 different terms from those listed here and write them in a logical order beside each number:

- full name
- education level
- age
- marital status
- height
- gang affiliation
- criminal history
- alcohol use

- nickname
- if Spanish is first language
- date of birth
- address
- weight
- identification
- ever arrested
- medical problems

- is the person literate
- speak any English
- place of birth
- phone number
- nationality
- profession
- drug use
- medication

Part II: Write your name on the paper and trade with a partner. Have your partner look for the questions in this section that would be used to obtain this information. Remember to take into consideration the gender of the person you will interview for certain questions (reference the name on the paper). It is not necessary to write the questions out, however, do practice them aloud in Spanish. After both of you are comfortable with saying the phrases in Spanish, interview one another using the questions you have both prepared. Don't forget to use the lead-in phrases from the beginning of this section to let the person you will interview know who you are and what is happening. Reference *Chapter 14* for help with letters and numbers when answering questions.

C) Cognates

Instructions: In Spanish, there are many words that are *cognates*. A *cognate* is a word that looks similar in Spanish to the English word and has the same meaning. In this section you have encountered quite a few such words. These words are extremely beneficial in learning a second language since they are easier to remember and understand. Below are some more *cognates*. Try to figure out what the English word is and write it in the blank beside of it. Ask your instructor to assist with the Spanish pronunciation. Then go back through previous sections and search for more *cognates*. Share what you find with classmates.

prisión = _____　　accidente = _____　　convicto = _____

fatalidad = _____　　hostil = _____　　tráfico = _____

Cyber-Investigation

Building upon the information you read in **BEFORE YOU BEGIN**, find information regarding a Hispanic immigrant's average level of education, typical profession and/or professions and socioeconomic background. How might this information assist you in dealing with Hispanics you encounter on and off of your job? Does this information vary greatly depending upon the immigrant's country of origin? Explain, why or why not.

Chapter 3

Physical and Personal Descriptions

Before You Begin

The term *Hispanic* does not refer to race but rather to a person whose culture and language are derived from Spanish America or Spain. Such an individual may be black, Asian, Caucasian, a native of the Americas, mestizo (Caucasian and native American ancestry) or mulatto (black and Caucasian ancestry). Therefore, when using the term *Hispanic America (Hispanoamérica [ee-spah-noh-ah-may-ree-kah])*, only those countries whose culture and language derived from Spain are included. However, when using the term *Latin America (América Latina [ah-may-ree-kah lah-tee-nah]* or *Latinoamérica [lah-tee-noh-ah-may-ree-kah]*), all other countries, such as Brazil (settled by Portugal), Haiti and others settled by France, are being included.

Moreover, the United States government created the classification *Hispanic (hispano/a [ee-spah-noh/nah])* in the early 1970s. The term was intended to classify the diverse population with ties to the Spanish language and/or culture. It is used to describe people who were born in any Spanish-speaking country of the Americas, or those who can trace their lineage to Spain or Spanish territories. This entails a large number of people from diverse countries and ethnic groups. However, it is important to note that many Hispanics would rather classify themselves according to their own national identity. This accounts for the distinct pride in associating oneself with one's country of origin rather than being lumped together under one general classification.

Phrases

English	Pronunciation & Spanish
1. What are you/is he/is she like?[1]	**koh**-moh ays? ¿Cómo es?
2. What were you/was he/was she like?[1]	**koh**-moh **ay**-rah? ¿Cómo era?
3. You are (not)/He is (not)/She is (not)[1] ...	(noh) ays ... (No) es ...
4. I was (not)/you were (not)/he was (not)/ she was (not) ... [1]	(noh) **ay**-rah ... (No) era ...
5. (the) man	(ayl) **ohm**-bray (el) hombre
6. (the) woman	(lah) moo-**hayr** (la) mujer
7. (the) child	(ayl/lah) **neen**-yoh/yah (el/la) niño/a[2]
8. (the) teen	(ayl/lah) ah-doh-lay-**sayn**-tay (el/la) adolescente[2]

9. (the) adult

*(ayl/lah) ah-**dool**-toh/tah*
(el/la) adulto/a[2]

10. (not) (very) young

*(noh) (moo^ee) **hoh**-bayn*
(no) (muy) joven

11. (not) (very) old

*(noh) (moo^ee) **bee^ay**-hoh/hah*
(no) (muy) viejo/a[3,4]

12. heavy

***groo^ay**-soh/sah*
grueso/a[4,5]

13. thin, slim

*dayl-**gah**-doh/dah*
delgado/a[4,6]

14. average sized

*day tah-**mahn**-yoh may-**dee^ah**-noh*
de tamaño mediano

15. white

***blahn**-koh/kah*
blanco/a[4]

16. black

***nay**-groh/grah*
negro/a[4]

17. dark-skinned

*day pee^ayl moh-**ray**-nah*
de piel morena

18. light-skinned

*day pee^ayl **klah**-rah*
de piel clara

19. blonde

***rroo**-bee^oh/ah*
rubio/a[4]

20. brunette/brown headed

*moh-**ray**-noh/nah*
moreno/a[4]

21. red headed

*pay-lee-**rroh**-hoh/hah*
pelirrojo/a[4]

22. tall

***ahl**-toh/tah*
alto/a[4]

23. short

***bah**-hoh/hah*
bajo/a[4]

24. Hispanic

*ee-**spah**-noh/nah*
hispano/a[4]

25. Asian

*ah-see-**ah**-tee-koh/kah*
asiático/a[4]

26. Indian

***een**-dee^oh/ah*
indio/a[4]

27. attractive

*ah-trahk-**tee**-boh/bah*
atractivo/a[4]

28. ugly	*fay*-oh/ah feo/a[4]	
29. bald	*kahl*-boh/bah calvo/a[4]	
30. You (don't) have/He (doesn't have) has / She (doesn't have) has … hair. [1]	(noh) *tee^ay*-nay ayl **pay**-loh … (No) tiene el pelo …	
long	*lahr*-goh. largo.	
short	*kohr*-toh. corto.	
curly	rree-*sah*-doh. rizado.	
straight	*lah*-see^oh. lacio.	
gray	kah-*noh*-soh. canoso.	
shaved [buzz cut]	rrah-*pah*-doh. rapado.	
black	*nay*-groh. negro.	
wavy	ohn-doo-*lah*-doh. ondulado.	
31. You (don't) have/He (doesn't have) has/ She (doesn't have) has … [1]	(noh) *tee^ay*-nay … (No) tiene …	
a moustache.	bee-*goh*-tay. bigote.	
a beard.	*bahr*-bah. barba.	
a goatee.	pay-*ree*-tah. perita.	
a pony tail/(pig tails).	koh-*lay*-tah(s). coleta(s).	
braids.	*trayn*-sahs. trenzas.	
a wig/toupee.	pay-*loo*-kah. peluca.	
braces (on teeth).	fray-*nee*-yohs. frenillos.	

dentures.	*dayn-tah-**doo**-rah poh-**stee**-sah.* dentadura postiza.
jewelry.	***hoh^ee**-yahs.* joyas.
side burns.	*pah-**tee**-yahs.* patillas.
acne.	***ahk**-nay.* acne.
a scar.	*see-kah-**trees.*** cicatriz.
a birth mark.	*ahn-**toh**-hoh.* antojo.
freckles.	***pay**-kahs.* pecas.
mole.	*loo-**nahr.*** lunar.
tattoo.	*tah-**too^ah**-hay.* tatuaje.
some type of deformity.	*ahl-**goo**-nah day-fohr-mee-**dahd.*** alguna deformidad.
weapon.	***ahr**-mah.* arma.[7]
32. You had (didn't have)/He had (didn't have)/She had (didn't have)…[1]	*(noh) tay-**nee**-ah …* (No) tenía …
33. You are (not)/He is (not)/She is (not)…[1]	*(noh) ays …* (No) es …
smart.	*een-tay-lee-**hayn**-tay.* inteligente.
stupid.	***tohn**-toh / tah.* tonto/a.[4]
lazy.	*pay-ray-**soh**-soh / sah.* perezoso/a.[4]
hard-working.	*trah-bah-hah-**dohr**(-ah).* trabajador/a.[5]
nice.	*seem-**pah**-tee-koh / kah.* simpático/a.[4]
unpleasant/mean.	*ahn-tee-**pah**-tee-koh / kah.* antipático/a.[4]

happy. [normally a happy person]	*fay-**lees.*** feliz.
crazy.	***loh**-koh/kah.* loco/a.⁴
good. [of good moral character]	***boo^ay**-noh/nah.* bueno/a.⁴
bad. [of poor moral character]	***mah**-loh/la* malo/a.⁴
clever/cunning.	***lee**-stoh/stah.* listo/a.⁴
34. You (don't) seem / He (doesn't seem)/ She (doesn't) seem … ¹	*(noh) ay-**stah** …* (No) está …
35. You seemed (didn't seem)/ He seemed (didn't seem)/ She seemed (didn't seem)…¹	*(noh) ay-**stah**-bah …* (No) estaba …
content/happy. [in a happy mood]	*kohn-**tayn**-toh/tah.* contento/a.⁴
sad.	***tree**-stay.* triste.
angry.	*ay-noh-**hah**-doh/dah.* enojado/a.⁴
nervous.	*nayr-**bee^oh**-soh/sah.* nervioso/a.⁴
anxious.	*ahn-**see^oh**-soh/sah.* ansioso/a.⁴
surprised.	*sohr-prayn-**dee**-doh/dah.* sorprendido/a.⁴
36. Are there/Were there any	*ah^ee/ah-**bee**-ah oo-nahs* ¿Hay/Había unas
distinctive markings	***mahr**-kahs dee-steen-**tee**-bahs* marcas distintivas
on the person's body?	*ayn ayl **koo^ayr**-poh day lah payr-**sohn**-nah?* en el cuerpo de la persona?
37. Where?	***dohn**-day?* ¿Dónde?
38. Can you draw it for me on this paper?	*may lahs **poo^ay**-day dee-boo-**hahr** ayn **ay**-stay pah-**payl**?* ¿Me las puede dibujar en este papel?

	ays …
39. You are/He is/She is …	Es …
	dee^ay-stroh/strah.
right handed.	diestro/a. [4]
	soor-doh/dah.
left handed.	zurdo/a. [4]

Notes

[1] In Spanish, unlike in English, the personal pronouns are rarely necessary. For this reason, one verb may have a variety of inferred persons or things attached to it. Context will typically clarify who or what is the subject of the verb. In such cases where you wish to indicate *you, he,* or *she,* a simple hand gesture toward the person to or of whom you are speaking will assist in clarification. Otherwise, you may include the person's name, whether the person is male or female *(hombre* or *mujer)* and then continue with your statement. For example: *"La mujer, ¿cómo era?" - "The woman, what was she like?"*

[2] Use *el (ayl)* and the *-o ending* (when the option is given) when referring to a *male,* use *la (lah)* and the *–a ending* (when the option is given) when referring to a *female.*

[3] The word *viejo/a* does mean *old* and can refer to people or things. However, when speaking about people, the word *mayor (mah^ee-yohr)* is more courteous. Understand that both are commonly heard.

[4] Use *-o* when describing a *male* and *-a* when describing a *female.*

[5] The word *grueso/a* literally means *thick* and is a polite term used to describe heavy/obese people. The word *gordo/a (gohr-doh/dah)* means *fat* and although not necessarily polite, it is also common in describing a persons stature. Note also that *gordo/a* may be used as a term of endearment among people who are close to one another. In such a case, it does not refer to a person's stature but rather only expresses an endearing sentiment.

[6] The word *delgado/a* is not a synonym for the word *flaco/a (flah-koh/kah)* which means *skinny* or *extremely thin/slim.*

[7] Reference *Chapter 7 – Threats, Dangers and Alerts – Weapons* for names of specific weapons.

Practical Activities

A) "He was a tall dark ... wait, or was it She?"

Instructions: In the last chapter, you learned to make the necessary changes in a phrase when addressing a *male* or a *female*. You now understand the importance of making such a distinction, especially in descriptions of a potential thief, attacker, etc. Below are descriptions of various persons. Using these clues, create the description in Spanish, making the appropriate changes to reflect gender when necessary and using complete phrases that are found in this section. Feel free to work in pairs or in small groups for this activity. After you have finished, share your Spanish descriptions with other pairs or groups to see if all of you agree. Be sure to make any necessary corrections.

person #1	*person #2*	*person #3*	*person #4*
teen male	young female	not very old male	old female
average size	very thin and tall	heavy and short	thin / average height
white	Hispanic	Asian	dark-skinned
redhead	brunette	ugly	gray hair
short hair	long and wavy hair	bald	braids
sideburns	jewelry	moustache / beard	glasses

B) "A little more detail, please."

Instructions: Building upon the skills you are acquiring from this section and the previous activity, you are going to learn how to make more detailed comments and questions. To do so, you will need to reference *Chapter 18 – The Body – Parts of the Body*. Before attempting this activity, review this chapter and the proper pronunciation for the parts of the body. Remember, it is not necessary to memorize them at this moment, but only to be able to find them and reference them as you need them. In the future, however, it would be a good a idea to learn the one's you most commonly use and how to manipulate them according to this activity. Once you have reviewed the referenced chapter, practice putting together the following phrases aloud in Spanish. A formula and sample sentences have been provided for you. Write out your desciptions in Spanish if you would like, but make sure to say them aloud and compare them with a classmate's to check for accuracy.

Formula and samples:

—/ *La mujer* / *El hombre** + *tiene (has)* / *tenía (had)* + *(mark)* + *en* + *su* + *(body part)*.

—*	tenía	antojo	en	su	frente.
You	had	a birthmark	on	your	forehead.

La mujer	tiene	lunar	en	su	naríz.**
She / The woman	has	a mole	on	her	nose.

El hombre	tenía	tatuaje	en	su	brazo derecho.
He / The man	had	a tatoo	on	his	right arm.***

* By excluding *La mujer* or *El hombre* and making eye contact with the person to whom you are speaking, *you* is implied.

** In Spanish, body parts are not typically personalized. Explanation would be lengthy and require the memorization of unnecessary information . Therefore, for the sake of simplicity, using *su (your/his/her)* is acceptable since it will not hinder communication. The plural of *su* is *sus* and would be used if referencing a plural body part, such as *hombros (shoulders)*.

*** In Spanish, normally, a description comes after the noun. For example *right (derecho) arm (brazo)* in Spanish is *brazo derecho* not *derecho brazo*. Gender will play a part in this, so have your instructor assist you if you have trouble.

1. The teenage girl had acne on her shoulders.

_____

2. The young man has freckles on his cheeks.

_____

3. The old, Asian woman had jewelry on her left wrist.

_____

4. The redheaded teenage boy has side burns and a scar on his right ear.

_____

Clothing, Accessories and Colors

Before You Begin

This section includes the most common and universally understood words for *articles of clothing* (*prendas de vestir [prayn-dahs day bay-steer]* in Spanish). Keep in mind that usage may vary depending upon the style or design of the article of clothing and in some instances within the region itself. This may be due to climate, culture and/or external influences. In the case that some types of clothing are trendy, it is not unusual to hear slang terminology, brand names or even the English words themselves used.

Persons already familiar with the Spanish language will not the omission of definite and indefinite articles in this entire chapter. Grammatically speaking, it would be more correct to incorporate them in the questions and statements you will be forming. However, for ease and manageability of the material for complete novices, they have been omitted and will not affect the intelligibility of your oral communication.

Phrases

English	Pronunciation & Spanish
1. You (don't) wear/ He (doesn't wear) wears/ She (doesn't wear) wears ...	*(noh) **yay**-bah ...* (No) lleva ... [1,2,3]
2. You were (not) wearing/ He was (not) wearing/ She was (not) wearing ...	*(noh) yay-**bah**-bah ...* (Noh) llevaba ... [2,3]
3. hat	*sohm-**bray**-roh* sombrero
4. earphones	*ah^oo-ree-koo-**lah**-rays* auriculares
5. glasses	***gah**-fahs* gafas
6. eye patch	***pahr**-chay ayn ayl **oh**-hoh* parche en el ojo
7. earring(s)	*ah-**ray**-tay(s)* arete(s)
8. necklace(s)	*koh-**yahr**(-ays)* collar(es)
9. watch(es)	*rray-**loh**(-hays)* reloj(es)
10. ring(s)	*ah-**nee**-yoh(s)* anillo(s)
11. shirt [with collar]	*kah-**mee**-sah* camisa

12. t-shirt [or shirt with no collar]	*kah-mee-**say**-tah* camiseta
13. pants	*pahn-tah-**loh**-nays* pantalones
14. shorts	*pahn-tah-**loh**-nays **kohr**-tohs* pantalones cortos
15. socks	*kahl-say-**tee**-nays* calcetines
16. (dress) shoes	*sah-**pah**-tohs (day bay-**steer**)* zapatos (de vestir)
17. athletic shoes	*sah-**pah**-tohs day **tay**-nees* zapatos de tenis
18. sandals	*sahn-**dah**-lee^ahs* sandalias
19. jacket	*chah-**kay**-tah* chaqueta
20. underwear	***rroh**-pah een-tay-**ree**^ohr* ropa interior
21. bra	*soh-**stayn*** sostén
22. (panty)hose/stockings	*(pahn-tee-)**may**-dee^ahs* (panti)medias
23. gloves	***goo**^ahn-tays* guantes
24. coat	*ah-**bree**-goh* abrigo
25. skirt	***fahl**-dah* falda
26. dress	*bay-**stee**-doh* vestido
27. suit	***trah**-hay* traje
28. uniform	*oo-nee-**fohr**-may* uniforme
29. tie	*kohr-**bah**-tah* corbata
30. bow tie	*pah-hah-**ree**-tah* pajarita[4]
31. blouse	***bloo**-sah* blusa

32. bracelet	*pool-**say**-rah* pulsera	
33. scarf	*boo-**fahn**-dah* bufanda	
34. bandana/handkerchief	*pahn-**oo^ay**-loh* pañuelo	
35. vest	*chah-**lay**-koh* chaleco	
36. long sleeved	*day **mahn**-gahs **lahr**-gahs* de mangas largas	
37. short sleeved	*day **mahn**-gahs **kohr**-tahs* de mangas cortas	
38. sleeveless	*seen **mahn**-gahs* sin mangas	
39. What color?	*day kay koh-**lohr**?* ¿De qué color?	
40. beige	*bay^eesh* beige	
41. olive green	*oh-**lee**-bah* oliva	
42. cream	***kray**-mah* crema	
43. khaki	***kah**-kee* caqui	
44. tan	*day kah-**fay klah**-roh* de café claro	
45. [other colors] [5]	*day . . .* de . . .	
gray	*grees* gris	
white	***blahn**-koh* blanco	
black	***nay**-groh* negro	
brown	*mah-**rrohn*** marrón	
blue	*ah-**sool*** azul	
purple	*moh-**rah**-doh* morado	

green

bayr-day
verde

yellow

*ah-mah-**ree**-yoh*
amarillo

orange

*ah-nah-rahn-**hah**-doh*
anaranjado

red

***rroh**-hoh*
rojo

pink

*rroh-**sah**-doh*
rosado

silver [either the metal or color]

*day **plah**-tah*
de plata

gold [either the metal or color]

*day **oh**-roh*
de oro

---

46. [add to color] …

light

***klah**-roh*
claro

dark

*oh-**skoo**-roh*
oscuro

---

47. solid

*day oon **soh**-loh koh-**lohr***
de un sólo color

---

48. (horizontal/vertical) stripes

*day rrah^**ee**-yahs (oh-ree-sohn-**tah**-lays/bayr-tee-**kah**-lays)*
de rayas (horizontales/verticales)

---

49. plaid

*day **koo^ah**-drohs*
de cuadros

---

50. printed

*day **tay**-lah ay-stahm-**pah**-dah*
de tela estampada

---

51. Did he/she cover his/her face with …

*say koo-**bree**-ah lah **kah**-rah kohn …*
¿Se cubría la cara con … [2]

a bandana/handkerchief?

*pahn-**oo^ay**-loh?*
pañuelo

a mask?

***mah**-skah-rah?*
máscara?

a stocking?

***may**-dee^ah?*
media?

some other object?

***oh**-troh ohb-**hay**-toh?*
otro objeto?

Notes

[1] Unlike English, the simple present tense in Spanish can also be used progressively. For example, *lleva* can mean *you are wearing, he is wearing* or *she is wearing*. Keep this in mind when you wish to ask someone a question such as *"Is she wearing a green scarf?"* which you can simply ask as *"La mujer, ¿lleva bufanda de verde?"*

[2] In Spanish, unlike in English, the personal pronouns are rarely necessary. For this reason, one verb may have a variety of inferred persons or things attached to it. Context will typically clarify who or what is the subject of the verb. In such cases where you wish to indicate *you, he,* or *she,* a simple hand gesture toward the person to or of whom you are speaking will assist in clarification. Otherwise, you may include the person's name, whether the person is male or female *(hombre* or *mujer)* and then continue with your statement. For example: *"La mujer, llevaba ..."* meaning, *"The woman, she was wearing ..."*

[3] You can also use these statements as *yes (sí [see])* or *no (no [noh])* questions by inflecting your voice at the end of the phrase and adding an article of clothing. For example: *"La mujer, ¿llevaba una bufanda?"* - *"The woman, was she wearing a scarf?"*

[4] You may also hear the word *moño (**mohn**-yoh)* for *bow tie.*

[5] This is not the most common way to describe the color of an item in Spanish. However, this method is the simplest since it does not require the speaker to worry about learning grammar rules for number, gender and adjective placement.

Practical Activities

Clothing, Accessories and Colors

A) "What was he/she wearing?"

Instructions: In the last section of this chapter, you learned to describe people physically and, somewhat, emotionally. In order to understand or give a more detailed description, it may be necessary to understand or give descriptions of the person's appearance, regarding clothing and accessories. Working either individually or with a partner, put together the following descriptions in Spanish. Make sure to say them aloud. You may write them out if you like, as well. Afterwards, check your descriptions with those of another person or pair and make any corrections. Make sure to review number 1 in the **Notes** for this section for clarification of *you, he* and *she.*

1.   He was wearing a blue suit, brown shoes, a white dress shirt and a red bow tie.

2.   She wears / is wearing a white and pink plaid skirt, a green, short-sleeved blouse and sandals.

3.   You were wearing an eye patch on your left eye, three* necklaces and two* rings on your right hand.**

 * Reference *Chapter 14 – The Basics – Numbers* if necessary.
** You will need to reference *Chapter 18 – The Body – Parts of the Body*. Also, remember that in Spanish, the description comes after the noun. For example *right (derecho) arm (brazo)* in Spanish is *brazo derecho* not *derecho brazo.*

B) Matching

Instructions: Match the English description on the left with the correct Spanish description on the right. Review your answers as a class when you have finished.

English	Spanish
1. __ olive green and black athletic shoes	a. camisa de rayas de anaranjado y verde
2. __ a long sleeve, light gray t-shirt	b. gafas de amarillo y rojo
3. __ a dark blue and cream print dress	c. zapatos de tenis de oliva y negro
4. __ silver and gold bracelets and earrings	d. abrigo y guantes de marrón oscuro
5. __ an orange and green striped collared shirt	e. pulseras y aretes de plata y de oro
6. __ a tan vest and a purple bandanna	f. camiseta de gris claro de mangas largas
7. __ a dark brown coat and gloves	g. vestido de tela estampada de azul oscuro y crema
8. __ yellow and red glasses	h. chaleco de café claro y pañuelo de morado

C) Putting It All Together

Part I - Instructions: Combining the information from both sections of *Chapter 3*, write in English, using only the phrases and expressions used in this chapter, a full description of a person. Make sure to include the following:

From the previous section:

- height / stature
- possible race
- approximate age group
- 2 descriptions of hair
- 2 identifying traits
- how the suspect may appear to be
- type of weapon the person had

From the current section:

- garment worn on torso including color(s), sleeve length, etc.
- garment worn on lower extremities, including color(s), etc.
- type of shoes worn on feet, including color(s), etc.
- 3 accessories worn by the person including, color(s) and part of the body
- item the person used to cover his / her face

Part II: Once you have the full description written in English, write you name on it and trade with a partner. Once you have received your partner's English description, it will be your task to compose the oral Spanish description. Feel free to consult the Spanish expressions in this chapter to assist you. Again, if you like, write out the Spanish description or make notes to help you remember what to say.

Part III: After everyone has had a chance to come up with their own Spanish description, form groups of four to five people and take turns saying your descriptions to the other members. Try your best to say as much as possible without having to look at the Spanish (rely on the English version to help you remember the Spanish phrases and expressions). Ask the members of your group to write down as much information in English as they can while they listen to you deliver the description in Spanish. If necessary, repeat the Spanish description. Afterwards, ask the group what they understood and verify their responses by checking your English description. Take turns doing this until everyone in the group has had a chance to recite his / her Spanish description.

Chapter 4

Useful Commands[1]

Phrases

English	Pronunciation & Spanish
1. Speak.	*ah*-blay(n). Hable(n).
2. Listen.	ay-*skoo*-chay(n). Escuche(n).
3. Eat.	*koh*-mah(n). Coma(n).
4. Sleep.	*doo^ayr*-mah(n). Duerma(n).
5. Work.	trah-*bah*-hay(n). Trabaje(n).
6. Be quiet.	*kah*-yay(n)-say. Cálle(n)se.
7. Sit down.	*see^ayn*-tay(n)-say. Siénte(n)se.
8. Show me.	*moo^ay*-stray(n)-may. Muéstre(n)me.
9. Get up.	lay-*bahn*-tay(n)-say. Levánte(n)se.
10. Clean yourself up.	*leem*-pee^ay(n)-say. Límpie(n)se.
11. Put it here.	*pohn*-gah(n)-loh ah-*kee*. Pónga(n)lo aquí.
12. Give it to me.	*day(n)*-may-loh. Dé(n)melo.
13. Hurry up.	ah-*poo*-ray(n)-say. Apúre(n)se.
14. Faster.	mahs *rrah*-pee-doh. Más rápido.
15. Slower.	mahs *layn*-toh. Más lento.

16. Leave.	*bah*-yah(n)-say. Váya(n)se.	
17. Come here.	*bayn*-gah(n) ah-*kee*. Venga(n) aquí.	
18. Repeat (that).	rray-*pee*-tah(n) (*ay*-soh). Repita(n) (eso).	
19. Turn off the lights.	ah-*pah*-gay(n) lahs *loo*-says. Apague(n) las luces.	
20. Turn it off.	ah-*pah*-gay(n)-loh. Apágue(n)lo.	
21. Take it out.	*sah*-kay(n)-loh. Sáque(n)lo.	
22. Do it.	*ah*-gah(n)-loh. Hága(n)lo.	
23. Now.	ah-*oh*-rah. Ahora.	
24. Later.	mahs *tahr*-day. Más tarde.	
25. Stop. [physically come to a stop]	*pah*-ray(n). Pare(n).	
26. Wait.	ay-*spay*-ray(n). Espere(n).	
27. Look.	*mee*-ray(n). Mire(n).	
28. Run.	*koh*-rrah(n). Corra(n).	
29. Walk.	kah-*mee*-nay(n). Camine(n).	
30. Take it.	*toh*-may(n)-loh. Tóme(n)lo.	
31. Bend over.	een-*klee*-nay(n)-say. Inclíne(n)se.	
32. Spread them.	say-*pah*-ray(n)-lohs. Sepáre(n)los.	
33. Drop it.	soo^*ayl*-tay(n)-loh. Suélte(n)lo.	
34. Join them.	*hoon*-tay(n)-se kohn *ay*-yohs. Júnte(n)se con ellos.	

35. Answer me.	*kohn-**tays**-tay(n)-may.* Contéste(n)me.	
36. Hands up.	*__mah__-nohs ah-**rree**-bah.* Manos arriba.	
37. On your knees.	*ah-rroh-**dee**-yay(n)-say.* Arrodílle(n)se.	
38. Hands behind your head/back.	*__mah__-nohs day-**trahs** day lah kah-**bay**-sah/ay-**spahl**-dah.* Manos destrás de la cabeza/espalda.	
39. Hands where I can see them.	*__mah__-nohs **dohn**-day lahs **poo^ay**-doh bayr.* Manos donde las puedo ver.	
40. Pull over and stop.	*__ah__-gah(n)-say ah oon **lah**-doh ee **pah**-ray(n).* Hága(n)se a un lado y pare(n).	
41. Hands on the vehicle	*__mah__-nohs ayn ayl bay-**ee**-koo-loh* Manos en el vehículo	
(where I can see them).	*(**dohn**-day lahs **poo^ay**-doh bayr).* (donde las puedo ver).	
42. Spit it out.	*ays-**koo**-pah(n)-loh.* Escúpa(n)lo.	
43. Return to your cell	*__boo^ayl__-bah(n) ah soo **sayl**-dah.* Vuélva(n) a su celda.	
44. Turn around.	*day(n) **oo**-nah **boo^ayl**-tah.* Dé(n) una vuelta.[2]	

Notes

[1] The *"(n)"* in many of the commands given in this chapter indicate the possibility of a *singular form* and a *plural form*. For example, the command *"Speak"* appears as *"Hable(n)."* To tell one person *"Speak,"* use *"Hable."* If addressing two or more people use *"Hablen."*

[2] This command asks for a 360° turn. To get someone to do a 180° turn use *Dé(n) una media vuelta* [*day(n) oo-nah **may**-dee^ah **boo^ayl**-tah*].

Practical Activities

A) Oral Practice - Chain Effect

Instructions: For this activity, form groups of 3 to 5 people, depending upon the size of your class. Then, the instructor will assign the 44 commands from this chapter so that each group has approximately the same number but, of course, different commands. It is then the responsibility of each group and all of its members to thoroughly learn their assigned commands. To do this, have each group member be responsible for a phrase or set of phrases. That group member will then learn the phrases well enough to teach the other members of the group without relying on the text. Once each member has taught all of his/her phrases and the group itself has learned them relatively well, have each group then teach the other groups the phrases their members have learned. Thus, the chain effect begins with an inidividual learning a few phrases, teaching his/her other group members and finally, each group teaching the others. Since these are commands, it would be best to associate each command with the respective action, when possible, to facilitate retention.

B) Commands

Instructions: You may have noticed that the commands presented in this chapter are affirmative. However, you may need to use the negative form at some point. Following the examples below, write the negative forms of the affirmative commands given. To pronounce the negative command follow the pronunciation given for the affirmative form of the command you need and place *no (noh)* in the proper position. Your instuctor may also help you with this. Don't worry about accent marks since writing is not the primary focus. Look for a pattern in the following examples. Pay attention to what happens to **me, se** and **lo** when they are present. When you are finished, ask your instructor to review the correct responses with the class.

	AFFIRMATIVE		NEGATIVE
1.	Arrodíllese.		No **se** arrodille.
2.	Contésteme.		No **me** conteste.
3.	Póngalo aquí.		No **lo** ponga aquí.
4.	Cállese.		_____
5.	Muéstreme.		_____
6.	Démelo.	B E	No **me lo** dé.
7.	Hágalo.	C	_____
8.	Váyase.	O M	_____
9.	Camine.	E	No camine.
10.	Corra.	S	No corra.
11.	Espere.		No espere.
12.	Mire.		_____
13.	Coma.		_____
14.	Escuche.		_____
15.	Trabaje.		_____

C) Plural Commands

Instructions: In exercise B, you learned how to form negative commands. However, up until now, you may have been practicing commands that were directed toward a single person. Review the **NOTES** from this section which contain the explanation for forming plural commands. Then, manipulate the commands from exercise B, both affirmative and negative, to indicate a command that would be given to two or more people. Feel free to write them out below.

Affirmative	*Negative*
1. _____	1. _____
2. _____	2. _____
3. _____	3. _____
4. _____	4. _____
5. _____	5. _____
6. _____	6. _____
7. _____	7. _____
8. _____	8. _____
9. _____	9. _____
10. _____	10. _____
11. _____	11. _____
12. _____	12. _____
13. _____	13. _____
14. _____	14. _____
15. _____	15. _____

Chapter 5

Parole and Probation Specifics

Identifying Clients and Confirming Appointments

Before You Begin

Be aware that the date in Spanish is reversed from the date in English. In Spanish, you always begin with the day rather than with the month. Always clarify or ask for clarification of dates using a calendar if you are unsure. You may choose to use a calendar as a visual reference to make sure there is no miscommunication. Also be aware that a calendar written in Spanish will typically begin on Monday rather than Sunday. Here are a few examples of dates:

Spanish: The 25th of March of 2006 = 25/3/2006
English: March 25th, 2006 = 3/25/2006

Spanish: The 1st of April of 2006 = 1/4/2006
English: April 1st, 2006 = 4/1/2006

In this section, as well as the rest of this text, you will see the term *libertad condicional* used to mean *parole*. However, should the term *libertad condicional* pose a problem in comprehension, the lesser used term *probatoria (proh-bah-**toh**-ree^ah)* may prove useful. To express probation use *libertad vigilada*.

Phrases

English	Pronunciation & Spanish
1. Your release date is the — of —, —.[1]	*soo **fay**-chah day lee-bay-rah-**see^ohn** ays ayl —day —day—.* Su fecha de liberación es el —de —de—.
2. You will be eligible for parole the — of —, —. [1]	*say-**rah** ay-lay-**hee**-blay **pah**-rah lah lee-bayr-**tahd** kohn-dee-see^oh-**nahl*** Será eligible para la libertad condicional *ayl —day —day—.* el —de —de—.
3. You will (not) be on parole after your release.	*(noh) ay-stah-**rah** ayn lee-bayr-**tahd** kohn-dee-see^oh-**nahl** day-**spoo^ays** day* (No) estará en libertad condicional después de *soo lee-bay-rah-**see^ohn**.* su liberación.
4. You have an appointment with your probation/parole officer the — of — at —.[2] a —.	***tee^ay**-nay **see**-tah kohn soo* Tiene cita con su *ah-**hayn**-tay day lee-bayr-**tahd** kohn-dee-see^oh-**nahl** ayl — day —* agente de libertad condicional el — de — *ah —.* ah —.

5. You have to arrive on time.

*tee^ay-nay kay yay-**gahr** ah **tee^aym**-poh*
Tiene que llegar a tiempo

(No exceptions.)

*(seen ayk-sayp-**see^oh**-nays).*
(sin excepciones).

6. You may not miss this appointment

*noh **poo^ay**-day fahl-**tahr ay**-stah **see**-tah*
No puede faltar esta cita

for any reason.

*pohr koo^ahl-**kee^ayr** rrah-**sohn**.*
por cualquier razón.

7. If there is an absolute emergency,

*see ah^ee **oo**-nah ay-mayr-**hayn**-see^ah bayr-dah-**day**-rah,*
Si hay una emergencia verdadera,

you must call this number.

*ah day yah-**mahr** ah **ay**-stay **noo**-may-roh.*
ha de llamar a este número.

8. Understand there are

*ayn-**tee^ayn**-dah kay ah^ee*
Entienda que hay

severe consequences for

*kohn-say-**koo^ayn**-see^ahs say-**bay**-rahs pohr*
consecuencias severas por

missing your appointment.

*fahl-**tahr** soo **see**-tah.*
faltar su cita.

9. It is your responsibility to keep each and

*ays soo rray-spohn-sah-bee-lee-**dahd** ah-koo-**deer** ah **kah**-dah **oo**-nah day*
Es su responsabilidad acudir a cada una de

every appointment (no matter what).

*soos **see**-tahs (say^ah loh kay say^ah).*
sus citas (sea lo que sea).

10. Your parole officer is—.

*soo ah-**hayn**-tay day lee-bayr-**tahd** kohn-dee-see^oh-**nahl** ays—.*
Su agente de libertad condicional es—.

11. Here is …

*ah-**kee tee^ay**-nay …*
Aquí tiene …

the address.

*lah dee-rrayk-**see^ohn**.*
la dirección.

the phone number.

*ayl **noo**-may-roh day tay-**lay**-foh-noh.*
el número de teléfono.

12. Take this with you as proof of

***yay**-bay **ay**-stoh kohn-**see**-goh **koh**-moh **proo^ay**-bah day*
Lleve esto consigo como prueba de

your appointment.

*soo **see**-tah.*
su cita.

13. Your parole officer …

*soo ah-**hayn**-tay day lee-bayr-**tahd** kohn-dee-see^oh-**nahl** …*
Su agente de libertad condicional …

speaks (a little) Spanish.

***ah**-blah (oon **poh**-koh day) ay-spahn-**yohl**.*
habla (un poco de) español.

does not speak Spanish.

*noh **ah**-blah ay-spahn-**yohl**.*
no habla español.

14. An interpreter will (not) be provided.

*(noh) say ah-**rah** dee-spoh-**nee**-blay ah oon een-**tayr**-pray-tay.*
(No) se hará disponible a un intérprete.

---

15. Will you need an interpreter?

*nay-say-see-tah-**rah** ah oon een-**tayr**-pray-tay?*
¿Necesitará a un intérprete?

---

16. You will need to take your own

*nay-say-see-tah-**rah** yay-**bahr** ah soo **proh**-pee^oh*
Necesitará llevar a su propio

interpreter.

*een-**tayr**-pray-tay.*
intérprete.

---

17. Make sure to take ...

*ah-say-**goo**-ray-say day yay-**bahr** ...*
Asegúrese de llevar ...

1 form ...

***oo**-nah **fohr**-mah*
una forma

2 forms ...

*dohs **fohr**-mahs*
dos formas

3 forms ...

*trays **fohr**-mahs*
tres formas

of identification.

*day ee-dayn-tee-fee-kah-**see**^ohn.*
de identificación.

---

18. Report to the Programs Office.

*pray-**sayn**-tay-say ayn lah oh-fee-**see**-nah day proh-**grah**-mahs.*
Preséntese en la Oficina de Programas.

---

19. Once you arrive, check in

***oo**-nah bays kay **yay**-gay pray-**sayn**-tay-say*
Una vez que llegue, preséntese

(with the guard on duty).

*(ahl **goo**^ahr-dee^ah day **toor**-noh).*
(al guardia de turno).

---

20. They may search you.

***poo**^ay-day kay lay rray-**hee**-strayn.*
Puede que le registren.

---

21. Cooperate fully.

*koh-oh-**pay**-ray kohm-play-tah-**mayn**-tay.*
Coopere completamente.

---

22. Do you have any correspondence that

***tee**^ay-nay ahl-**goo**-nah **klah**-say day koh-rray-spohn-**dayn**-see^ah kay*
¿Tiene alguna clase de correspondencia que

verifies your appointment?

*bay-ree-**fee**-kay soo **see**-tah?*
verifique su cita?

---

23. With whom is your appointment?

*kohn kee^ayn **tee**^ay-nay soo **see**-tah?*
¿Con quién tiene su cita?

---

24. What time is your appointment?

*ah kay **oh**-rah ays soo **see**-tah?*
¿A qué hora es su cita?[2]

---

25. I need to verify your indentity.

*nay-say-**see**-toh bay-ree-fee-**kahr** soo ee-dayn-tee-**dahd**.*
Necesito verificar su identidad.

26. I need to see …	*nay-say-**see**-toh bayr …* Necesito ver …
1 form …	***oo**-nah **fohr**-mah* una forma
2 forms …	*dohs **fohr**-mahs* dos formas
3 forms …	*trays **fohr**-mahs* tres formas
of identification.	*day ee-dayn-tee-fee-kah-**see**^ohn.* de identificación.
27. Sign in here, please.	***feer**-may ah-**kee** pohr fah-**bohr**.* Firme aquí, por favor.
28. Wait …	*ay-**spay**-ray …* Espere …
here.	*ah-**kee**.* aquí.
there.	*ah-**yee**.* allí.
in the waiting area.	*ayn lah **sah**-lah day ay-**spay**-rah.* en la sala de espera.
until your name is called.	***ah**-stah kay **yah**-mayn soo **nohm**-bray.* hasta que llamen su nombre.
29. Cell phone use is not permitted.	*noh say payr-**mee**-tay ayl **oo**-soh dayl say-loo-**lahr**.* No se permite el uso del celular.
30. Food or drink is not permitted.	*noh say payr-**mee**-tay nee koh-**mee**-dah nee bay-**bee**-dah.* No se permite ni comida ni bebida.
31. No smoking.	*say proh-**ee**-bay foo-**mahr**.* Se prohíbe fumar.
32. Children are not permitted.	*noh say payr-**mee**-tay ah **neen**-yohs.* No se permite a niños.

Notes

[1] To say the date in Spanish, always use this formula: *el + (number) + de + (month) + de + (year) = "el 12 de agosto de 2010"* or *in English "the 12th of August, 2010."* Reference *Chapter 14 - The Basics - Numbers* for assistance with saying numbers in Spanish. See *Chapter 17 – Telling Time the Easy Way – Day, Months and Dates* for names of the days and months in Spanish.

[2] To include the time or be able to understand it, see *Chapter 17 – Telling Time the Easy Way* and *Chapter 14 – The Basics – Numbers*. When possible, you may simply prefer to write out this type of information for the Spanish speaker to avoid any misunderstandings.

Practical Activities
Identifying Clients and Confirming Appointments

A) Times and Dates

Instructions: Using the information given in the **Notes** for this section, practice saying the following appointment times and dates in Spanish. An example has been provided to help you get started. For quick reference, here are the formulas for saying the date and time:

$$date = el + (number) + de + (month) + de + (year);$$

$$time\ of\ an\ event\ (appointment) = a\ la/las + (number) + (time\ of\ day).$$

ex. The 5th of January, 2014 at 3 p.m. = El 5 de enero de 2014 a las 3 de la tarde.

1. The 1st of April, 2012 at 11 a.m.*

2. The 30 of November, 2029 at 12 p.m.

3. 09/17/2021 at 1:45 p.m.

4. The 18th of August, 2016 at 8 p.m.

5. The 26 of June, 2043 at 7:30 a.m.

6. 05/23/2019 at 10:15 a.m.

* Only the first day of a month uses the *ordinal number first* in Spanish: *primero (pree-may-roh)*. After *first*, Spanish uses *cardinal numbers (two, three, etc.)* unlike English.

B) Oral Practice

Instructions: You are arranging an appointment for a client to meet with his/her probation officer. In doing so, you must explain what the client can expect and what is expected of the client. Based on the clues given below, find the phrases and expressions in this section that would help you convey these instructions. Once you have finished, practice saying your instructions aloud, then pair up with a classmate and take turns giving each other the instructions in Spanish. When it is your turn to be the listener, try to comprehend as much of the Spanish as possible without looking in your text for assistance.

- client release date
- time and date of appointment with probation officer
- must arrive on time; cannot miss appointment or there are severe consequences
- responsibility for keeping every appointment, no matter what
- name of probation officer (create name); address and phone number
- take this document as proof of appointment
- probation officer does not speak Spanish; an interpreter will be provided
- take 2 forms of identification
- go to the Programs Office and report to the guard on duty
- you may be searched so cooperate
- wait in the waiting room until you are called
- no cell phones, food or drink are permitted

C) Phrase Fragments

Instructions: **Match the phrase fragments from the first column with those from the second column. After you have completed them all, practice saying each one aloud as a class and then give the English meaning.**

1. __ Estará eligible para la ...

a. a su propio intérprete.

2. __ Su agente de libertad condicional ...

b. correspondencia que verifique su cita?

3. __ Necesitará llevar ...

c. tiene su cita?

4. __ Asegúrese de ...

d. habla un poco de español.

5. __ ¿Tiene alguna clase de ...

e. 3 formas de identificación.

6. __ Firme aquí, ...

f. es su cita?

7. __ ¿Con quién ...

g. a un intérprete?

8. __ ¿Necesitará ...

h. por favor.

9. __ Necesito ver ...

i. libertad condicional el 3 de agosto de 2015.

10. __ ¿A qué hora ...

j. llevar 3 formas de indentificación.

Routine Office Procedures for Parole and Probation Officers

Before You Begin

In the Hispanic culture, the concept of time is relatively different. Punctualilty is not a great concern, and being late for events is considered socially acceptable. Since time is of great importance to your appointment scheduling make sure to reitierate policies and consequences regarding scheduling and keeping appointments with the appropriate expressions provided. Remember, if you are a probation officer simply replace "*condicional*" with "*vigilada*" where necessary.

Phrases

English	Pronunciation & Spanish
1. I'm your parole officer.	*soh^ee soo ah-**hayn**-tay day lee-bayr-**tahd** kohn-dee-see^oh-**nahl**.* Soy su agente de libertad condicional.
2. My name is—.	*may **yah**-moh—.* Me llamo—.
3. Follow me, please.	***see**-gah-may pohr fah-**bohr**.* Sígame, por favor.
4. Have a seat, please.	***see^ayn**-tay-say pohr fah-**bohr**.* Siéntese, por favor.
5. This is a copy in Spanish	***ay**-stah ays **oo**-nah **koh**-pee^ah ayn ay-spahn-**yohl*** Esta es una copia en español
of the conditions of parole.	*day lahs **nohr**-mahs day lah lee-bayr-**tahd** kohn-dee-see^oh-**nahl**.* de las normas de la libertad condicional.
6. Can you read them?	***poo^ay**-day lay-**ayr**-lahs?* ¿Puede leerlas?
7. (If not) I can read them to you.	*(see noh) say lahs **poo^ay**-doh lay-**ayr**.* (Si no) se las puedo leer.
8. Do you understand them?	*lahs ayn-**tee^ayn**-day?* ¿Las entiende?
9. It is imperative that you follow them	*ays eem-pay-rah-**tee**-boh kay lahs **see**-gah ahl pee^ay* Es imperativo que las siga al pie
exactly.	*day lah **lay**-trah.* de la letra.
10. There is no excuse for	*noh ah^ee neen-**goo**-nah ayk-**skoo**-sah pohr* No hay ninguna excusa por
not following them.	*noh say-**geer**-lahs.* no seguirlas.
11. Understand there are	*ayn-**tee^ayn**-dah kay ah^ee* Entienda que hay
extreme consequences	*kohn-say-**koo^ayn**-see^ahs **grah**-bays* consecuencias graves

for violating these conditions.	*pohr noh say-**geer** ay-stahs **nohr**-mahs.* por no seguir estas normas.
12. These are your program goals.	***ay**-stahs sohn soos **may**-tahs **pah**-rah **ay**-stay proh-**grah**-mah.* Estas son sus metas para este programa.
13. You will need to enroll in ...	*nay-say-see-tah-**rah** een-skree-**beer**-say ayn oon proh-**grah**-mah ...* Necesitará inscribirse en un programa ...
an adult study program.	*ay-doo-kah-**tee**-boh **pah**-rah ah-**dool**-tohs.* educativo para adultos.
vocational training.	*day kah-pah-see-tah-**see^ohn** boh-kah-see^oh-**nahl**.* de capacitación vocacional.
14. This is your work assignment.	***ay**-stah ays soo ah-seeg-nah-**see^ohn** day trah-**bah**-hoh.* Esta es su asignación de trabajo.
15. I need to ask you some questions.	*nay-say-**see**-toh ah-**sayr**-lay oo-nahs pray-**goon**-tahs.* Necesito hacerle unas preguntas.
16. Please respond yes or no when possible.	*rray-**spohn**-dah see oh noh **koo^ahn**-doh say^ah poh-**see**-blay pohr fah-**bohr**.* Responda sí o no cuando sea posible, por favor.
17. Will you live alone?	*bee-bee-**rah** **soh**-loh/lah?* ¿Vivirá solo/a?[1]
18. With whom will you live?	*kohn kee^ayn bee-bee-**rah**?* ¿Con quién vivirá?[2]
19. Will you work?	*trah-bah-hah-**rah**?* ¿Trabajará?
20. Where?	***dohn**-day?* ¿Dónde?
21. Will you write the information for me here?	*may ay-**skree**-bay lah een-fohr-mah-**see^ohn** ah-**kee**?* ¿Me escribe la información aquí?
22. You are (not) eligible for community volunteer passes.	*(noh) ays ay-lee-**hee**-blay **pah**-rah **pah**-says day boh-loon-**tah**-ree^oh.* (No) es eligible para pases de voluntario.
23. You will have to perform (#) hours of	*tayn-**drah** kay day-saym-payn-**yahr** (#) **oh**-rahs day* Tendrá que desempeñar (#) horas de
community service.	*sayr-**bee**-see^oh koh-moo-nee-**tah**-ree^oh.[3]* servicio comunitario.
24. You are (not) elegible for	*(noh) ays ay-lee-**hee**-blay **pah**-rah ayl proh-**grah**-mah day* (No) es eligible para el programa de
work release.	*rray-een-sayr-**see^ohn** lah-boh-**rahl**.* reinserción laboral.

25. Your custody level is ...

*soo nee-**bayl** day koo-**stoh**-dee^ah ays ...*
Su nivel de custodia es ...

    minimum.

*****mee**-nee-moh.*
mínimo.

    medium.

*may-**dee^ah**-noh.*
mediano.

    closed.

*say-**rrah**-doh.*
cerrado.

26. This means for you ...

*****ay**-stoh lay seeg-nee-**fee**-kah ...*
Esto le significa ...

    more/less supervision.

*mahs/**may**-nohs soo-payr-bee-**see^ohn**.*
más/menos supervisión.

    more/less freedom of movement.

*mahs/**may**-nohs lee-bayr-**tahd** day moh-bee-**mee^ayn**-toh.*
más/menos libertad de movimiento.

    limited personal property and

*proh-pee^ay-**dahd** payr-soh-**nahl** ee proh-grah-mah-**see^ohn***
propiedad personal y programación

      programming.

*lee-mee-**tah**-dahs.*
limitadas.

    more program opportunities.

*mahs oh-pohr-too-nee-**dah**-days day proh-grah-mah-**see^ohn**.*
más oportunidades de programación.

    participation in ...

*pahr-tee-see-pah-**see^ohn** ayn lohs*
participación en los ...

      community work programs.

*proh-**grah**-mahs day trah-**bah**-hoh koh-moo-nee-**tah**-ree^ohs.*
programas de trabajo comunitarios.

      partial imprisonment.

*rray-kloo-**see^ohn** pahr-**see^ahl**.*
reclusión parcial.

      escorted excursions.

*ayk-skoor-**see^oh**-nays kohn ay-**skohl**-tah.*
excursiones con escolta.

      a stay of — months.

*ay-**stahn**-see^ah day —**mays**(-ays).*
estancia de — mes(es).[3]

27. Your parole has (not) been approved.

*(noh) say lay ah kohn-say-**dee**-doh lah lee-bayr-**tahd** kohn-dee-see^oh-**nahl**.*
(No) se le ha concedido la libertad condicional.

28. Your parole will last — month(s).

*soo lee-bayr-**tahd** kohn-dee-see^oh-**nahl** doo-rah-**rah** —**mays**(-ays).*
Su libertad condicional durará — mes(es).[3]

29. Your next custody review will be

*soo **prohk**-see-mah ay-bah-loo-ah-**see^ohn** day koo-**stoh**-dee^ah say-**rah***
Su próxima evaluación de custodia será

    the — of —,—.

ayl —day —day—.
el —de —de—. [4]

30. This is the time and date of your	*ay-stahs sohn lah **oh**-rah ee lah **fay**-chah day soo* Estas son la hora y la fecha de su
next appointment with me/with your	***prohk**-see-mah **see**-tah kohn-**mee**-goh / kohn soo* próxima cita conmigo/con su
parole officer.	*ah-**hayn**-tay day lee-bayr-**tahd** kohn-dee-see^oh-**nahl**.* agente de libertad condicional.
31. Before you leave, you will need to take a	***ahn**-tays day **eer**-say tayn-**drah** kay soh-may-**tayr**-say ah oon* Antes de irse, tendrá que someterse a un
urine test.	*ah-**nah**-lee-sees day oh-**ree**-nah.* análisis de orina.
32. The urine test will look for drugs	*ayl ah-**nah**-lee-sees day oh-**ree**-nah day-tayk-tah-**rah droh**-gahs* El análisis de orina detectará drogas
or illegal substances.	*oh soo-**stahn**-see^ahs ee-lay-**gah**-lays.* o sustancias ilegales.

Notes

[1] Use -o when referring to a *male* and -a when referring to a *female*.

[2] See *Chapter 15 – Family and Friends* for Spanish terms.

[3] See *Chapter 14 – The Basics – Numbers* for pronunciation of numbers in Spanish.

[4] To say the date in Spanish, always use this formula: *el + (number) + de + (month) + de + (year)* = "*el 12 de agosto de 2010*" or *in English "the 12th of August, 2010."* Reference *Chapter 14 - The Basics - Numbers* for assistance with saying numbers in Spanish.

Practical Activities

Routine Office Procedures for Parole and Probation Officers

A) Oral Practice

Instructions: You are a probation/parole officer meeting with a client for the first time. First, form pairs with a classmate and decide who will meet with client A and who will meet with client B. Once clients have been assigned, individually review this section and find the appropriate phrases and expressions will need to convey the necessary information to your assigned client according to the specifications given. After you have prepared this information, practice saying it aloud in Spanish to your partner. When you are speaking, your partner should try to listen and comprehend as much information as possible without consulting the text.

Client A	Client B
• introduce yourself and state your name	• introduce yourself and state your name
• present a copy in Spanish of the conditions of probation/parole	• present a copy in Spanish of the conditions of probation/parole
• explain the importance of following them and that not doing so has consequences	• explain the importance of following them and that not doing so has consequences
• state program goals: enroll in vocational training	• state program goals: enroll in adult education
• give work assignment	• inform client you need to ask some questions

• tell client to respond yes or no to the following questions:
    work? (client answer: *yes*)
    where?
	• tell client to respond yes or no to the following questions:
	    live alone? (client answer: *yes*)
	    where?

• state client has a medium custody level	• state client has minimum custody level
• explain medium custody level specifics	• explain minimum custody level specifics
• provide the duration of probation/parole	• provide date of next custody review
• assign time and date of next appointment	• assign time and date of next appointment

B) Phrase Fragments

Instructions: Match the phrase fragments from the first column with those from the second column. After you have completed them all, practice saying each one aloud in pairs followed by the English meaning.

1. __ ¿Puede …   a. concedido la libertad condicional.

2. __ ¿Las …   b. detectará drogas o sustancias ilegales.

3. __ Se las …   c. entiende?

4. __ No se le ha …   d. excursiones con escolta.

5. __ Antes de irse, tendrá que someterse …   e. puedo leer.

6. __ El análisis de orina …   f. para este programa.

7. __ Estas son las hora y la fecha de …   g. leerlas?

8. __ Esto le significa …   h. la información aquí?

9. __ ¿Me escribe …   i. a un análisis de orina.

10. __ Estas son sus metas …   j. su próxima cita conmigo.

Cyber-Investigation

Do an Internet search for HISPANICS and PUNCTUALITY. Then compare and contrast their concept of time and punctuality with that of our mentality in the United States. How do they differ? Why do they differ? Are there any similarities?

Conditions of Probation[1] - English/Spanish and Phonetics[2]

Regular Conditions. – As regular conditions of probation, a defendant must:

Las normas de la libertad vigilada. - Según las normas de la libertad vigilada, el acusado debe de:

*[lahs **nohr**-mahs day lah lee-bayr-**tahd** bee-hee-**lah**-dah. - say-**goon** lahs **nohr**-mahs day lah lee-bayr-**tahd** bee-hee-**lah**-dah, ayl ah-koo-**sah**-doh **day**-bay day:]*

(1) Commit no criminal offense in any jurisdiction.

(1) cometer ningún delito criminal en ninguna jurisdicción.

*[koh-may-**tayr** neen-**goon** day-**lee**-toh kree-mee-**nahl** ayn neen-**goo**-nah hoo-rees-deek-**see**^ohn]*

(2) Remain within the jurisdiction of the court unless granted written permission to leave by the court or his probation officer.

(2) quedarse dentro de la jurisdicción de el tribunal a menos que le sea otorgado permiso escrito para salir por el tribunal (el juez) o el agente encargado de su libertad vigilada.

*[kay-**dahr**-say **dayn**-troh day lah hoo-rees-deek-**see**^ohn day ayl tree-boo-**nahl** ah **may**-nohs kay lay say^ah oh-tohr-**gah**-doh payr-**mee**-soh ay-**skree**-toh **pah**-rah sah-**leer** pohr ayl tree-boo-**nahl** (ayl hoo^ays) oh ayl ah-**hayn**-tay ayn-kahr-**gah**-doh day soo lee-bayr-**tahd** bee-hee-**lah**-dah]*

(3) Report as directed by the court or his probation officer to the officer at reasonable times and places and in a reasonable manner, permit the officer to visit him at reasonable times, answer all reasonable inquiries by the officer and obtain prior approval from the officer for, and notify the officer of, any change in address or employment.

(3) informarle a su agente según lo especificado por el tribunal (el juez) o el agente de libertad vigilada mismo de sus paraderos a horas y lugares razonables y de un modo razonable, hacerse disponible para reunirse con el agente a horas razonables, responder a toda pregunta razonable hecha por el agente, obtener aprobación de antemano del agente para, y darle a conocer al agente también de, cualquier cambio en su dirección o empleo.

*[een-fohr-**mahr**-lay ah su ah-**hayn**-tay say-**goon** loh ay-spay-see-fee-**kah**-doh pohr ayl tree-boo-**nahl** (ayl hoo^ays) oh ayl ah-**hayn**-tay day lee-bayr-**tahd** bee-hee-**lah**-dah **mees**-moh day soos pah-rah-**day**-rohs ah **oh**-rahs ee loo-**gah**-rays rrah-soh-**nah**-blays ee day oon **moh**-doh rrah-soh-**nah**-blay, ah-**sayr**-say dee-spoh-**nee**-blay **pah**-rah rray-oo-**neer**-say kohn ayl ah-**hayn**-tay ah **oh**-rahs rrah-soh-**nah**-blays, rray-spohn-**dayr** ah **toh**-dah pray-**goon**-tah rrah-soh-**nah**-blay **ay**-chah pohr ayl ah-**hayn**-tay, ohb-tay-**nayr** ah-proh-bah-**see**^ohn day ahn-tay-**mah**-noh dayl ah-**hayn**-tay **pah**-rah, ee **dahr**-lay ah koh-noh-**sayr** ahl ah-**hayn**-tay tahm-**bee**^ayn day, kwahl-**kee**^ayr **kahm**-bee^oh ayn soo dee-rayk-**see**^ohn oh aym-**play**-oh.]*

(4) Satisfy child support and other family obligations as required by the court. If the court requires the payment of child support, the amount of the payments shall be determined as provided in G.S. 50-13.4(c).

(4) cumplir con la obligación de manutención de niño y cualesquier otras obligaciones familiares mandadas por el tribunal (el juez). Si el tribunal requiere el pago de manutención de niño, se determinará la cantidad de los pagos según lo esbozado en el estatuto general 50-13.4(c).

*[koom-**pleer** kohn lah oh-blee-gah-see^**ohn** day mah-noo-tayn-see^**ohn** day **neen**-yoh ee koo^ah-lays-kee^**ayr** ohb-lee-gah-see^**ohn**-nays fah-mee-**lee**^**ah**-rays mahn-**dah**-dahs pohr ayl tree-boo-**nahl** (ayl hoo^ays). see ayl tree-boo-**nahl** rray-kee^**ay**-ray ayl **pah**-goh de mah-noo-tayn-see^**ohn** day **neen**-yoh, say day-tayr-mee-nah-**rah** lah kahn-tee-**dahd** day lohs **pah**-gohs say-**goon** loh ays-boh-**sah**-doh ayn ayl ay-stah-**too**-toh hay-nay-**rahl** seen-koo^**ayn**-tah, ghee-**ohn** tray-say **poon**-toh koo^**ah**-troh, say]*

(5) Possess no firearm, explosive device or other deadly weapon listed in G.S. 14-269 without the written permission of the court.

(5) tener en su posesión ninguna arma de fuego, ningún dispositivo explosivo ni cualquier otra clase de arma mortífera enumerada en el estatuto general 14-269 sin el permiso escrito de el tribunal (el juez).

*[tay-**nayr** ayn soo poh-say-see^**ohn** neen-**goo**-nah **ahr**-mah day **foo**^ay-goh, neen-**goon** dees-poh-see-**tee**-boh ayk-sploh-**see**-boh nee koo^ahl-**kee**^**ayr** oh-trah **klah**-say day **ahr**-mah mohr-tee-fay-rah ay-noo-may-rah-dah ayn ayl ay-stah-**too**-toh hay-nay-**rahl** kah-tohr-say, ghee-**ohn** doh-see^**ayn**-tohs say-**sayn**-tah ee **noo**^**ay**-bay seen ayl payr-**mee**-soh ay-skree-toh day ayl tree-boo-**nahl** (ayl hoo^ays)]*

(6) Pay a supervision fee as specified in subsection (c1).

(6) pagar los honorarios de supervisión descritos en la subdivisión (c1).

*[pah-**gahr** lohs oh-noh-**rah**-ree^ohs day soo-payr-bee-see^**ohn** day-skree-tohs ayn lah soob-dee-bee-see^**ohn** say oo-noh]*

(7) Remain gainfully and suitably employed or faithfully pursue a course of study or of vocational training that will equip him for suitable employment. A defendant pursuing a course of study or of vocational training shall abide by all of the rules of the institution providing the education or training, and the probation officer shall forward a copy of the probation judgment to that institution and request to be notified of any violations of institutional rules by the defendant.

(7) conseguir y permanecer en un trabajo lucrativo que le sea adecuado o seguir un curso de estudios o capacitación vocacional que lo preparará para un trabajo que le convenga. El acusado que sigue un curso de estudios o capacitación vocacional se adherirá a todas las reglas del instituto que dispone del programa educativo o de capacitación vocacional y el agente de libertad vigilada le enviará una copia de la decisión de la libertad vigilada a ese instituto y pedirá que se le notifique de cualesquier violaciones de las reglas institucionales cometidas por el acusado.

*[kohn-say-**geer** ee payr-mah-nay-**sayr** ayn oon trah-**bah**-hoh loo-krah-**tee**-boh kay lay say^ah ah-day-koo^**ah**-doh oh say-**geer** oon **kohr**-soh day ay-stoo-dee^ohs oh kah-pah-see-tah-see^**ohn** boh-kah-see^oh-**nahl** kay loh pray-pah-rah-**rah** pah-rah oon trah-**bah**-hoh kay lay kohn-**bayn**-gah. ayl ah-koo-**sah**-doh kay **see**-gay oon **koor**-soh day ay-stoo-dee^ohs oh kah-pah-see-tah-see^**ohn** boh-kah-see^oh-**nahl** say ahd-ay-ree-**rah** ah toh-dahs lahs rray-glahs dayl een-stee-too-toh kay dee-**spoh**-nay dayl proh-**grah**-mah ay-doo-kah-**tee**-boh oh day kah-pah-see-tah-see^**ohn***

*boh-kah-see^oh-**nahl** ee ayl ah-**hayn**-tay day lee-bayr-**tahd** bee-hee-**lah**-dah lay ayn-bee^ah-**rah** oo-nah koh-pee^ah day lah day-see-**see^ohn** day lah lee-bayr-**tahd** bee-hee-**lah**-dah ah **ay**-say een-stee-**too**-toh ee pay-dee-**rah** kay say lay noh-tee-**fee**-kay day koo^ah-lays-**kee^ayr** bee^oh-lah-**see^oh**-nays day lahs **rray**-glahs een-stee-too-see^oh-nah-lays koh-may-**tee**-dahs pohr ayl ah-koo-**sah**-doh]*

(8) Notify the probation officer if he fails to obtain or retain satisfactory employment.

(8) informarle al agente de libertad vigilada si el acusado fracasa en obtener o retener empleo satisfactorio.

*[een-fohr-**mahr**-lay ahl ah-**hayn**-tay day lee-bayr-**tahd** bee-hee-**lah**-dah see ayl ah-koo-**sah**-doh frah-**kah**-sah ayn ohb-tay-**nayr** oh rray-tay-**nayr** aym-**play**-oh sah-tees-fahk-**toh**-ree^oh]*

(9) Pay the costs of court, any fine ordered by the court, and make restitution or reparation as provided in subsection (d).

(9) pagar las costas procesales, cualquier multa impuesta por el tribunal (el juez) y hacer restitución o reparación según lo descrito en la subdivisión (d).

*[pah-**gahr** lahs **koh**-stahs proh-say-**sah**-lays, koo^ahl-**kee^ayr mool**-tah eem-**poo^ay**-stah pohr ayl tree-boo-**nahl** (ayl hoo^ays) ee ah-**sayr** rray-stee-too-**see^ohn** oh rray-pah-rah-**see^ohn** say-**goon** loh day-**skree**-toh ayn lah soob-dee-bee-**see^ohn** day]*

(10) Pay the State of North Carolina for the costs of appointed counsel, public defender, or appellate defender to represent him in the case(s) for which he was placed on probation.

(10) pagarle al estado de Carolina del Norte las costas para la designación de un abogado, defensor público o defensor de apelaciones para representarle en los casos por los cuales se le concedió la libertad vigilada.

*[pah-**gahr**-lay ahl ay-**stah**-doh day kah-roh-**lee**-nah dayl **nohr**-tay lahs **koh**-stahs **pah**-rah lah day-seeg-nah-see^ohn day oon ah-boh-**gah**-doh, day-fayn-**sohr poo**-blee-koh oh day-fayn-**sohr** day ah-pay-lah-see^oh-nay **pah**-rah rray-pray-sayn-**tahr**-lay ayn lohs **kah**-sohs pohr lohs koo^ah-lays say lay kohn-say-dee-**oh** lah lee-bayr-**tahd** bee-hee-**lah**-dah]*

(11) At a time to be designated by his probation officer, visit with his probation officer at a facility maintained by the Division of Prisons. In addition to these regular conditions of probation, a defendant required to serve an active term of imprisonment as a condition of special probation pursuant to G.S. 15A-1344(e) or G.S. 15A-1351(a) shall, as additional regular conditions of probation, obey the rules and regulations of the Department of Correction governing the conduct of inmates while imprisoned and report to a probation officer in the State of North Carolina within 72 hours of his discharge from the active term of imprisonment.

(11) visitar con el agente de libertad vigilada designado en un sitio mantenido por la División de Prisiones a la hora programada por el agente de libertad vigilada. Además de estas normas de la libertad vigilada, un acusado que ha de cumplir una condena activa como parte de una libertad vigilada excepcional conforme al estatuto general 15A-1334(e) o el estatuto general 15A-1351 (a), obedecerá, como normas adicionales a las ya vigentes, las reglas y los reglamentos del Departamento de Correcciones que supervisa la conducta de los presos mientras que están encarcelados y le hará saber a un agente de libertad vigilada del estado de Carolina del Norte dentro de 72 horas de la liberación del acusado al cumplir su condena.

*[bee-see-**tahr** kohn ayl ah-**hayn**-tay day lee-bayr-**tahd** bee-hee-**lah**-dah day-seeg-**nah**-doh ayn oon **see**-tee^oh mahn-tay-**nee**-doh pohr lah dee-bee-**see**^ohn day pree-**see**^oh-nays ah lah **oh**-rah proh-grah-**mah**-dah pohr ayl ah-**hayn**-tay de lee-bayr-**tahd** bee-hee-**lah**-dah. ah-day-**mahs** day **ay**-stahs **nohr**-mahs day lah lee-bayr-**tahd** bee-hee-**lah**-dah, oon ah-koo-**sah**-doh kay ah day koom-**pleer** oo-nah kohn-**day**-nah ahk-**tee**-bah **koh**-moh **pahr**-tay day oo-nah lee-bayr-**tahd** bee-hee-**lah**-dah ayk-sayp-see^oh-**nahl** kohn-**fohr**-may ahl ay-stah-**too**-toh hay-nay-**rahl** **keen**-say ah ghee-**ohn**, meel, tray-see^**ayn**-tohs **tray**^een-tah ee **koo**^ah-troh ay, oh **keen**-say ah, ghee-**ohn**, meel, tray-see^**ayn**-tohs seen-**koo**^ayn-tah ee oo-noh ah, oh-bay-day-say-**rah**, **koh**-moh **nohr**-mahs ah-dee-see^oh-**nah**-lays ah lahs yah bee-**hayn**-tays, lahs **rray**-glahs ee lohs rray-glah-**mayn**-tohs dayl day-pahr-tah-**mayn**-toh day koh-rrayk-see^**oh**-nays kay soo-payr-**bee**-sah lah kohn-**dook**-tah day lohs **pray**-sohs **mee**^ayn-trahs kay ay-**stahn** ayn-kahr-say-**lah**-dohs ee lay ah-**rah** sah-**bayr** a oon ah-**hayn**-tay day lee-bayr-**tahd** bee-hee-**lah**-dah dayl ay-**stah**-doh day kah-roh-**lee**-nah dayl **nohr**-tay **dayn**-troh day say-**tayn**-tah ee dohs **oh**-rahs day lah lee-bay-rah-see^**ohn** dayl ah-koo-**sah**-doh ahl koom-**pleer** soo kohn-**day**-nah]*

Regular conditions of probation apply to each defendant placed on supervised probation unless the presiding judge specifically exempts the defendant from one or more of the conditions in open court and in the judgment of the court. It is not necessary for the presiding judge to state each regular condition of probation in open court, but the conditions must be set forth in the judgment of the court.

Las normas de la libertad vigilada le aplican a cada acusado bajo lo pautado por la libertad vigilada a no ser que el juez que preside exonere específicamente al acusado de uno o más de las normas en un tribunal abierto y en el juicio de el tribunal. No es menester que el juez que preside lea en voz alta cada una de las normas de la libertad vigilada en un tribunal abierto, sin embargo, hay que establecer las normas durante el juicio de el tribunal.

*[lahs **nohr**-mahs day lah lee-bayr-**tahd** bee-hee-**lah**-dah lay ah-**plee**-kahn ah **kah**-dah ah-koo-**sah**-doh **bah**-hoh loh pah^oo-**tah**-doh pohr lah lee-bayr-**tahd** bee-hee-**lah**-dah ah noh sayr kay ayl hoo^ays kay pray-**see**-day ayk-soh-**nay**-ray ay-spay-see-fee-kah-**mayn**-tay ahl ah-koo-**sah**-doh day oo-noh oh mahs day lahs **nohr**-mahs ayn oon tree-boo-**nahl** ah-bee^**ayr**-toh ee ayn ayl **hoo**^ee-see^oh day ayl tree-boo-**nahl**. noh ays may-nay-**stayr** kay ayl hoo^ays kay pray-**see**-day **lay**-ah ayn bohs **ahl**-tah **kah**-dah oo-nah day lahs **nohr**-mahs day la lee-bayr-**tahd** bee-hee-**lah**-dah ayn oon tree-boo-**nahl** ah-bee^**ayr**-toh seen aym-**bahr**-goh ah^ee kay ay-stah-blay-**sayr** lahs **nohr**-mahs doo-**rahn**-tay ayl **hoo**^ee-see^oh day ayl tree-boo-**nahl**]*

Defendants placed on unsupervised probation are subject to the provisions of this subsection, except that defendants placed on unsupervised probation are not subject to the regular conditions contained in subdivisions (2), (3), (6), (8), and (11).

Los acusados bajo la libertad no vigilada se ven sujetos a los reglamentos de esta subdivisión, salvo que los bajo la libertad no vigilada no son sujetos a las normas pautadas en las subdivisiones (2), (3), (6), (8) y (11).

*[lohs ah-koo-**sah**-dohs **bah**-hoh lah lee-bayr-**tahd** noh bee-hee-**lah**-dah say bayn soo-**hay**-tohs ah lohs rray-glah-**mayn**-tohs day **ay**-stah soob-dee-bee-see^**ohn**, **sahl**-boh kay lohs **bah**-hoh lah lee-bayr-**tahd** noh bee-hee-**lah**-dah noh sohn soo-**hay**-tohs ah lahs **nohr**-mahs pah^oo-**tah**-dahs ayn lahs soob-dee-bee-see^**oh** -nays dohs, trays, say^ees, oh-choh ee **ohn**-say]*

Notes

[1] No specific activities have been created for this section. However, practicing the phonetics by reading this section aloud is highly recommended and will facilitate the initial reading of longer phrases and expressions throughout the text.

[2] English version obtained from *http://ncga.state.nc.us/EnactedLegislation/SessionLaws/PDF/1993-1994/SL1994-9es.pdf*

Please be aware that this translation is state specific. It is intended as a sample document only to provide guidance in assisting the person conveying the information. Of course, cited statutes will vary as well as some content depending upon the state. Make sure to reference the statutes of your respective state.

Chapter 6

Drug/Alcohol Inquiries and Procedures

Before You Begin

The difficulties associated with assimilation into the American culture and way of life make Hispanic immigrants in the United States more likely to use illegal drugs and to abuse alcohol. Assimilated Hispanics were nearly twice as likely as non-assimilated Hispanics to report binge drinking and more than three times as likely to report consuming alcohol continuously for days in a row without sobering up. Although immigration and cultural assimilation may provide some people with better income and job stability, it is nonetheless a difficult process that may have unforeseen consequences.

Phrases

English	Pronunciation & Spanish
1. I need to see …	*nay-say-**see**-toh bayr …* Necesito ver …
your license.	*soo lee-**sayn**-see^ah day kohn-doo-**seer**.* su licencia de conducir. [1]
proof of vehicle registration.	***proo^ay**-bah day mah-tree-koo-lah-**see^ohn** dayl bay-**ee**-koo-loh.* prueba de matriculación del vehículo.
proof of vehicle insurance.	***proo^ay**-bah day say-**goo**-roh dayl bay-**ee**-koo-loh.* prueba de seguro del vehículo.
2. Have you been drinking (taking drugs)?	*ah ay-**stah**-doh toh-**mahn**-doh (**droh**-gahs)?* ¿Ha estado tomando (drogas)? [2]
3. Are you …	*ay-**stah** …* ¿Está …
drunk?	*boh-**rrah**-choh/chah?* borracho/a? [3]
high?	*pah-**sah**-doh/dah?* pasado/a? [3]
hung over?	*kohl-**gah**-doh/dah?* colgado/a? [3]
4. Are you diabetic?	***tee^ay**-nay dee^ah-**bay**-tays?* ¿Tiene diabetes?

5. Do you have any mental/physical problems?	*tee^**ay**-nay ahl-**goon** proh-**blay**-mah mayn-**tahl**/**fee**-see-koh?* ¿Tiene algún problema mental/físico?
6. Do you take medication?	***toh**-mah may-dee-**see**-nah?* ¿Toma medicina?
7. Do you know where you are?	***sah**-bay **dohn**-day ay-**stah**?* ¿Sabe dónde está?
8. Do you suffer from seizures?	***soo**-fray day ah-**tah**-kays/kohn-bool-**see^oh**-nays?* ¿Sufre de ataques/convulsiones?
9. Have you taken/drank a lot or a little?	*ah toh-**mah**-doh **moo**-choh oh **poh**-koh?* ¿Ha tomado mucho o poco? [2]
10. Don't fall asleep.	*noh say **doo^ayr**-mah.* No se duerma.
11. Show me what you took.	***moo^ay**-stray-may loh kay toh-**moh**.* Muéstreme lo que tomó.
12. Please step out of the vehicle.	*fah-**bohr** day bah-**hahr** dayl bay-**ee**-koo-loh.* Favor de bajar del vehículo.
13. Please stay in your vehicle.	*fah-**bohr** day payr-mah-nay-**sayr** ayn ayl bay-**ee**-koo-loh.* Favor de permanecer en el vehículo.
14. Stand up.	***pohn**-gah-se day pee^ay.* Póngase de pie.
15. Do (exactly) what I do.	***ah**-gah (ayk-sahk-tah-**mayn**-tay) loh kay **ah**-goh yoh.* Haga (exactamente) lo que hago yo.
16. Where did you get this?	*day **dohn**-day ohb-**too**-boh **ay**-stoh?* ¿De dónde obtuvo esto?
17. Who gave/sold it to you?	*kee^ayn say loh dee^oh/bayn-**dee^oh**?* ¿Quién se lo dio/vendió?
18. How much did it cost?.	***koo^ahn**-toh koh-**stoh**?* ¿Cuánto costó? [4]
19. Who is the dealer?	*kee^ayn ays ayl droh-**gay**-roh?* ¿Quién es el droguero?
20. Give me all that you have.	*ayn-**tray**-gay-may **toh**-doh loh kay **tee^ay**-nay.* Entrégueme todo lo que tiene.
21. Empty your pockets.	*bah-**see**-ay lohs bohl-**see**-yohs.* Vacíe los bolsillos.
22. Show me your hands.	***moo^ay**-stray-may lahs **mah**-nohs.* Muéstreme las manos.
23. Lie face down/up and don't move.	*ah-**koo^ays**-tay-say **boh**-kah ah-**bah**-hoh/ah-**rree**-bah ee noh say **moo^ay**-bah.* Acuéstese boca abajo/arriba y no se mueva.

24. Interlace your fingers

    *ayn-tray-**lah**-say lohs **day**-dohs*
    Entrelace los dedos

    (behind your back/neck).

    *(day-**trahs** day lah ay-**spahl**-dah/lah **noo**-kah).*
    (detrás de la espalda/la nuca).

25. Kneel.

    *ah-rroh-**dee**-yay-say.*
    Arrodíllese.

26. I am going to ...

    boh^ee ah ...
    Voy a ...

    frisk you.

    *rray-hee-**strahr**-lay.*
    registrarle.

    cuff you.

    *ays-poh-**sahr**-lay.*
    esposarle.

    search the cell.

    *rray-hee-**strahr** lah **sayl**-dah.*
    registrar la celda.

    arrest you.

    *ah-rray-**stahr**-lay.*
    arrestarle.

    take you home.

    *yay-**bahr**-lay ah **kah**-sah.*
    llevarle a casa.

    take your fingerprints.

    *toh-**mahr**-lay lahs **oo^ay**-yahs dee-hee-**tah**-lays/dahk-tee-**lah**-rays.*
    tomarle las huellas digitales/dactilares.

    give you a ticket.

    *dahr-lay **oo**-nah **mool**-tah.*
    darle una multa.

    give you a warning (this time).

    *dahr-lay oon ah-**bee**-soh (**ay**-stah bays).*
    darle un aviso (esta vez).

27. I don't have anything.

    *noh **tayn**-goh **nah**-dah.*
    No tengo nada.

28. Is this yours?

    *ays **soo**-yoh?*
    ¿Es suyo?

29. Whose is this?

    day kee^ayn ays?
    ¿De quién es?

30. Return to your cell.

    ***boo^ayl**-bah ah soo **sayl**-dah.*
    Vuélva a su celda.

31. Don't let this happen again.

    *noh **day**-hay kay **ay**-stoh **pah**-say day **noo^ay**-boh.*
    No deje que esto pase de nuevo.

32. Let's go.

    ***bah**-mohs.*
    Vamos.

33. All substance possession is prohibited.

    *say proh-**ee**-bay lah poh-say-**see^ohn** day **toh**-dah soo-**stahn**-see^ah*
    Se prohíbe la posesión de toda sustancia

    *ee- **lee**-see-tah.*
    ilícita.

34. Substance possession is	*lah poh-say-**see**^ohn day soo-**stahn**-see^ahs ee-**lee**-see-tahs ays* La posesión de sustancias ilícitas es
punishable by law.	*kah-stee-**gah**-blay pohr lay^ee.* castigable por ley.

35. It is illegal …	*ays ee-lay-**gahl** …* Es ilegal …
to drink and drive.	*toh-**mahr** ee mah-nay-**hahr**.* tomar y manejar.[1]
to have open containers in a	*tay-**nayr** ayn-**bah**-says ah-**bee**^ayr-tohs day ahl-koh-**ohl** ayn oon* tener envases abiertos de alcohol en un
vehicle.	*bay-**ee**-koo-loh.* vehículo.

Notes

[1] Remember, *manejar (mah-nay-**hahr**)* is synonymous with *conducir (kohn-doo-seer)*.

[2] The verb *tomar (toh-**mahr**)* is used to express *to drink (alcohol)* and *to take (drugs)*. Used without the word *drogas*, it infers the use of *alcohol*, whereas used with the word *drogas*, it states clearly the use of *drugs*.

[3] Use *-o* when referring to *males* and *-a* when referring to *females*.

[4] Have the person write the answer for you if you have trouble comprehending the oral response.

Practical Activities

A) Oral Practice

Instructions: Tell and/or ask the individuals indicated below the following information. Make sure to pay attention to the gender of the person to whom you are speaking.

Addressing:	You ask/say:	Individual responds:
Adult male	Have you been drinking?	Yes.
	Have you been taking drugs?	No.
	Are you drunk?	A little.
	Have you drank a little or a lot?	Not much. *(no mucho – noh moo-choh)*
	Do you know where you are?	No.
	Show me your hands.	—
	Lie face down and don't move.	—
	Interlace your fingers behind your neck.	—
	I am going to arrest you.	—
Adult female	Are you high?	A little.
	Show me what you took.	—
	Where did you get this?	I don't know.*(no sé – noh say)*
	Empty your pockets.	—
	Kneel and interlace your fingers behind your back.	—
	I am going to cuff you	—
	Stand up. Let's go.	—

B) Translation

Instructions: Below are instructions that were given to a Spanish speaking driver that was stopped at a routine check point. Translate this information aloud or in writing into English. Try to do as much as you can without having to look back at this section. After you have finished, check your translation against the meanings of the phrases and expressions in this section.

Necesito ver su licencia de conducir y prueba de matriculación del vehículo ... Favor de bajar de su vehículo ... Haga exactamente lo que hago yo ... Vacíe los bolsillos y muéstreme las manos ... Voy a registrarle ... Es ilegal tener envases abiertos de alcohol en un vehículo ... Voy a darle un aviso esta vez pero (but) no deje que esto pase de nuevo.

C) What would you say?

Instructions: For each of the situations below, give examples of three to four phrases or expressions the public safety official would use from this chapter. Share what you would say with a classmate and explain why the phrases/expressions you chose would be appropriate.

1. A state trooper stops a car that is swerving and notices the driver is wearing a medical alert necklace.
2. A corrections officer finds an inmate barely conscious and sees a small plastic baggy in his hand.
3. A police officer stops to question someone suspected of having an ilicit substance on his/her person.

Cyber-Investigation

Understandably, cultural assimilation can be quite difficult. It may not only impact a person physically but mentally as well. Search the Internet for challenges that Hispanics face upon immigrating into the U. S.? How do these challenges impact the individual? Their family? What resources are available to assist these people when they find themselves in difficult situations? Share your findings with the class.

Narcotics, Stimulants and Other Drugs[1]

Before You Begin

In Spanish, the word *droga (**droh**-gah)* does not refer to *medicine (medicina [may-dee-see-nah])* but rather refers to narcotics and illegal drugs. Also, the word *drogaría (droh-gah-ree-ah)* is a *false cognate* – it looks like an English word but does not mean what one may think. Instead of being a place to buy *drogas*, it is a store that sells all other types of products, from shampoo and soap to cleaning products. Only a *farmacia* (which is a cognate for the word *pharmacy [fahr-**mah**-see^ah])* would sell *medicina*.

Phrases

English	Pronunciation & Spanish
1. Show me what you have.	*moo^**ays**-tray-may loh kay **tee^ay**-nay.* Muéstreme lo que tiene.
2. Those are ...	*sohn ...* Son ... [2]
3. Are those ... ?	*sohn ... ?* ¿Son ... ? [2]
4. I don't know.	*noh say.* No sé.
5. narcotic(s)	*nahr-**koh**-tee-koh(s)* narcótico(s)
6. stimulant(s)	*ays-tee-moo-**lahn**-tay(s)* estimulante(s)
7. depressant(s)	*say-**dahn**-tay(s)* sedante(s)[3]
8. cannabis	*kah-**nah**-bees* canabis
9. inhalant(s)	*een-ah-**lahn**-tay(s)* inhalante(s)
10. hallucinogen(s)	*ah-loo-see-**noh**-hay-noh(s)* alucinógeno(s)
11. (ilegal) drugs	***droh**-gahs (ee-lay-**gah**-lays)* drogas (ilegales)
12. cocaine	*koh-kah-**ee**-nah* cocaína
13. opium	***oh**-pee^oh* opio

14. crack	*krahk* crack
15. heroin	*ay-roh-**ee**-nah* heroína
16. crank	*krahnk* crank
17. morphine	*mohr-**fee**-nah* morfina
18. psilocybin	*see-loh-see-**bee**-nah* silocibina
19. nicotine	*nee-koh-**tee**-nah* nicotina
20. caffeine	*kah-fay-**ee**-nah* cafeína
21. amphetamine(s)	*ahn-fay-tah-**mee**-nah(s)* anfetamina(s)
22. dexedrine	*dayk-stroh-ahn-fay-tah-**mee**-nah* dextroanfetamina
23. benzadrine	*bayn-say-**dree**-nah* bencedrina
24. LSD (acid)	***ah**-see-doh* ácido
25. mescaline	*mays-kah-**lee**-nah* mescalina
26. peyote	*pay-**yoh**-tay* peyote
27. methedrine	*may-tahn-fay-tah-**mee**-nah* metanfetamina
28. alcohol	*ahl-koh-**ohl*** alcohol
29. tuinal	*too^ee-**nahl*** tuinal
30. hashish	*ah-**sheesh*** hashish
31. tranquilizer(s)	*trahn-kee-lee-**sahn**-tay(s)* tranquilizante(s)
32. barbituate(s)	*bahr-bee-**too**-ree-koh(s)* barbitúrico(s)

33. marijuana	*mah-ree-**hoo^ah**-nah* marijuana
34. sleeping pill(s)	*pah-**stee**-yah(s) **pah**-rah dohr-**meer*** pastilla(s) para dormir
35. seconal	*say-koh-**nahl*** seconal
36. glue	*pay-gah-**mayn**-toh* pegamento
37. sedative(s)	*say-**dahn**-tay(s)* sedante(s)
38. ether	***ay**-tayr* éter
39. nitrous oxide	***ohk**-see-doh nee-**troh**-soh* óxido nitroso
40. gasoline	*gah-soh-**lee**-nah* gasolina
41. PCP	*pay say pay* PCP
42. paint thinner	***tee**-nayr* tiner

43. Do you …

sniff/huff?	*een-**ah**-lah?* inhala?
shoot up?	*say een-**yayk**-tah?* se inyecta?
snort?	*ah-**spee**-rah?* aspira?
chew coca?	*koh-**kay**-ah?* coquea?
smoke?	***foo**-mah?* fuma?
chip?	*kohn-**soo**-may **droh**-gahs een-fray-koo^ayn-tay-**mayn**-tay?* consume drogas infrecuentemente?
deal?	***bayn**-day **droh**-gahs?* vende drogas?
free-base?	*koo-**kay**-ah?* cuquea?
use drugs?	***oo**-sah **droh**-gahs?* usa drogas?

44. What drugs do you use?	*kay **droh**-gahs **oo**-sah?* ¿Qué drogas usa?	
45. angel dust	***pohl**-boh day **ahn**-hayl* polvo de angel	
46. quaaludes	***loo**-dees* ludis	
47. red devils	*dee^**ah**-blohs **rroh**-hohs* diablos rojos	
48. roach	*koh-**lee**-yah* colilla	
49. joint	***frah**-hoh* frajo	
50. crystal	*kree-**stahl*** cristal	
51. dime bag	***dah^ee**-may* daime	
52. nickel bag	***nee**-klay* nicle	
53. whites	***blahn**-kahs* blancas	
54. speed	*payp* pep	
55. smack	***stoo**-fah* stufa	
56. shrooms	***ohn**-gohs **mah**-hee-kohs* hongos mágicos	
57. crack	*bah-**soo**-koh* basuco	
58. stash	*ay-skohn-**dee**-tay day **droh**-gahs* escondite de drogas	
59. It was an overdose (of …).	*foo^ay **oo**-nah soh-bray-**doh**-sees (day …).* Fue una sobredosis (de …).	
60. Did you/he/she overdose (on …)?	*say dee^oh **oo**-nah **doh**-sees ayk-say-**see**-bah (day …)?* ¿Se dio una dosis excesiva (de …)?	

Notes

[1] This section provides many popular terms. Please be aware that such terms frequently change and sometimes using the proper name for the drug instead of the popular term may be the clearest way to convey your message. The popular terms are provided primarily to assist you in recognizing words you may hear.

[2] Notice these two expressions in Spanish are the same. The vocal inflection (in a question, raising the pitch of the voice at the end of a phrase slightly) and context in which they are used will distinguish their usage. The singular forms of these two expressions are *Es ... (This is ...)* and *¿Es ... ? (Is this ... ?)* —both pronounced *ays*. Once again, since they are the same word, vocal inflection will determine whether you make a statement or a question.

[3] The word *calmante (kahl-**mahn**-tay)* can also mean *depressant* as well as *tranquilizer (tranquilizante [trahn-kee-lee-**sahn**-tay]).*

Practical Activities

Narcotics, Stimulants and Other Drugs

A) Question or Statement

Instructions: Below are English questions or statements that you must translate into Spanish. Once you have translated each item, form pairs with a classmate and practice saying each one according to its classification as a question or statement. Remember vocal inflection is important to make the distinction.

1. These are narcotics.

2. Is this cannabis?

3. This is an amphetamine.

4. Are these barbiturates?

5. These are sedatives.

6. Is this crack?

7. Are these red devils?

8. This is smack.

B) Getting More Information

Instructions: You are talking to a person you suspect of substance possession. Read the following situation, then plan what you would say to the individual in Spanish. You may need to review the previous section of this chapter for additional information. When you have finished, form small groups of 4 to 5 people and tell your group members what you would say in Spanish, explaining the context as you. Once you have done this, pair up with a classmate and practice being the suspect for each other. Recreate each other's situation entirely in Spanish with both of you speaking Spanish dialogue. Have your instructor assist you with the suspect's Spanish answers if necessary.

Situation: You are talking to an individual and must find out if he/she is carrying, using and/or distributing illicit substances. You suspect this person is high and continue by asking what the individual has, if the individual is a substance user and what drugs he/she uses. Lastly, you instruct the individual to empty his/her pockets and notice a strange packet, you open it and find (choose substance from vocabulary) inside. Inquire as to what they are/it is and ask how he/she uses it. Finally tell the person, he/she is being arrested and explain that possession is illegal.

Cyber-Investigation

You are probably well aware of the problems with Latin American drug-trafficking. Undoubtedly, the problem is pervasive and no single Latin American country carries all of the blame. Research which countries are most involved and what substance/substances they are responsible for trafficking. What measures are being taken by the U. S. to combat Latin American drug-trafficking? How well are these measures working? What would you do differently, or do you believe the U. S. government is doing everything possible?

Administering a Urine Test[1]

Phrases

English	Pronunciation & Spanish
1. You will have to provide a urine sample.	*tayn-drah kay proh-bay-ayr oo-nah moo^ay-strah day oh-ree-nah.* Tendrá que proveer una muestra de orina.
2. Please verify your personal information	*pohr fah-bohr bay-ray-fee-kay soo een-fohr-mah-see^ohn payr-soh-nahl* Por favor, verfique su información personal
(on this container).	*(ayn ay-stay frah-skoh).* (en este frasco).
3. Take this container to the restroom and	*yay-bay-say ayl frah-skoh ahl bahn-yoh ee* Llévese el frasco al baño y
fill it (up to here) with urine.	*yay-nay-loh (hoo-stoh ah-stah ah-kee) kohn oh-ree-nah.* llénelo (justo hasta aquí) con orina.
4. I will have to watch you urinate into	*tayn-dray kay bayr-lay oh-ree-nahr ayn* Tendré que verle orinar en
the container.	*ayl frah-skoh.* el frasco.
5. She will/he will have to watch you	*tayn-drah kay bayr-lay* Tendrá que verle
urinate into the container.	*oh-ree-nahr ayn ayl frah-skoh.* orinar en el frasco.[2]
6. Do not close the door	*noh see^ay-rray lah poo^ayr-tah* No cierre la puerta
(or flush the toilet).	*(nee tee-ray day lah kah-day-nah dayl ee-noh-doh-roh).* (ni tire de la cadena del inodoro).
7. Before urinating, clean your genitals	*ahn-tays day oh-ree-nahr leem-pee^ay-say bee^ayn lohs hay-nay-tah-lays* Antes de orinar, límpiese bien los genitales
with this.	*kohn ay-stoh.* con esto.
8. Then, begin to urinate into the toilet.	*ayn-tohn-says koh-mee^ayn-say ah oh-ree-nahr ayn ayl ee-noh-doh-roh.* Entonces, comience a orinar en el inodoro.[2]
9. Then, urinate into the container.	*ayn-tohn-says oh-ree-nay ayn ayl frah-skoh.* Entonces, orine en el frasco.
10. Afterwards, leave it …	*day-spoo^ays loh bah ah day-hahr …* Después, lo va a dejar …
with me.	*kohn-mee-goh.* conmigo.

with the corrections officer.	*kohn ayl/lah ah-**hayn**-tay day koh-rrayk-**see^oh**-nays.* con el/la agente de correcciones.[4]
with that person.	*kohn **ay**-sah payr-**soh**-nah.* con esa persona.

Notes

[1] In the case that you should need to order a blood test, use the following phrase:

I am going to order a blood test	*boh^ee ah pay-**deer** oon ah-**nah**-lee-sees day **sahn**-gray* Voy a pedir un análisis de sangre
to check for alcohol/drugs.	***pah**-rah day-tayk-**tahr** ahl-koh-**ohl** / **droh**-gahs.* para detectar alcohol/drogas.

[2] Since third person Spanish verb conjugations can be ambiguous (meaning *he, she, you, they,* etc.), make a simple hand gesture toward the person in reference here to clarify who will be observing.

[3] This phrase has been included if a mid-stream urine test is required.

[4] Use *la* if you know the person in reference is a *female*, otherwise use *el*, which references a *male* or the *agente* in a general manner.

Practical Activities

Administering a Urine Test

A) Oral Practice

Instructions: Using only Spanish, give a classmate these necessary instructions as if he/she were a Spanish-speaking inmate, suspect, etc..

- Tell him/her, a urine sample will need to be provided, but first, to verify his/her personal information on the container. Then, take the container to the restroom.

- Instruct the person not to close the door or flush the toilet and that you will have to watch him/her urinate into the container. Finally, tell him/her to leave the sample with you.

B) Matching

Instructions: Match the beginning of each phrase from the first column with the correct ending from the second column. Then practice saying each phrase aloud and providing the English meaning.

1.___ Llévese el frasco al baño y . . .   a. con el agente de correcciones.

2. ___ Antes de orinar, . . .   b. de sangre para detectar drogas.

3. ___ Después, lo va a dejar . . .   c. orinar en el inodoro.

4. ___ Voy a pedir un análisis . . .   d. orine en el frasco.

5. ___ Entonces, . . .   e. ni tire de la cadena del inodoro.

6. ___ Entonces, comience a . . .   f. llénelo justo hasta aquí con orina.

7. ___ No cierre la puerta . . .   g. verle orinar en el frasco.

8. ___ Tendrá que . . .   h. límpiese bien los genitales con esto.

Follow-up

Instructions: Aloud, individually or as a class, put the phrases from the matching activity that deal with a *urine test* in the most logical order.

Chapter 7

Threats, Dangers and Alerts[1,2]

Before You Begin

Disclaimer—The first two sections in this chapter contain explicit material and are provided solely for reference. The decision to include these expressions and phrases was based on the polling of focus group participants who are public safety professionals. Please be advised, it is not expected that you will practice these expressions and phrases with the intention to use them but rather to understand them. This will benefit you greatly in knowing whether there is a potential safety risk for yourself as well as anyone around you. When possible, variations for individual phrases are provided, but as with slang and popular speech in any language, their usage may quickly become obsolete. Also, be aware, that a native speaker's knowledge of such terminology will vary greatly by generation, socioeconomic status, regional language differences, and possibly gender.

Phrases

English	Pronunciation & Spanish
1. Grab him/her.	*ah-**gah**-rrah-loh/lah.* Agárralo/la. ***koh**-hay-loh/lah.* Cógelo/la.
2. Grab the gun.	*ah-**gah**-rrah lah pee-**stoh**-lah.* Agarra la pistola. ***koh**-hay-lay lah pee-**stoh**-lah.* Cógele la pistola. ***cheen**-gah-lay lah pee-**stoh**-lah / ayl **koo^ay**-tay.* Chíngale la pistola / el cuete.
3. Grab him by the balls.	*ah-**gah**-rrah-lay pohr lohs **oo^ay**-bohs.* Agárrale por los huevos.
4. Here he/she comes.	*ah-**kee bee^ay**-nay.* Aquí viene.
5. Take his/her head off.	*ah-**rrahn**-kah-lay lah kah-**bay**-sah.* Arráncale la cabeza.
6. Finish him/her off.	*ah-**kah**-bah kohn ayl / **ay**-yah.* Acaba con él / ella.

83

7. Jump him/her.

breen-kah-loh/lah.
Bríncalo/la.

8. Careful/Watch out.

*koo^ee-**dah**-doh.*
Cuidado.

troo-chah.
Trucha.

***oh**-hoh.*
Ojo.

9. Cut him/her.

***kohr**-tah-loh/lah.*
Córtalo/la.

***pee**-kah-loh/lah.*
Pícalo/la.

10. Fuck him/her up.

***cheen**-gah-loh/lah.*
Chíngalo/la.

11. When he's/she's not looking,

*koo^**ahn**-doh say days-koo^**ee**-day*
Cuando se descuide,

we'll get him/her.

*loh / lah ah-gah-**rrah**-mohs.*
lo/la agarramos.

*koo^**ahn**-doh say **bee**-ray loh/lah breen-**kah**-mohs.*
Cuando se vire, lo/la brincamos.

12. Cut off his balls.

***kohr**-tah-lay lohs oo^**ay**-bohs.*
Córtale los huevos.

*days-koh-**hoh**-nah-loh.*
Descojónalo.

*days-**oo^ay**-bah-loh*
Deshuévalo.

13. Grab the damn thing.
[most likely a weapon]

***cheen**-gah-lay lah cheen-gah-**day**-rah.*
Chíngale la chingadera.

14. Kill him/her.

***dah**-lay ayn lah **mah**-dray.*
Dale en la madre.

***hoh**-day-loh/lah.*
Jódelo/la.

*ay-lee-**mee**-nah-loh/lah.*
Elimínalo/la.

***leen**-cha-loh/lah.*
Línchalo/la.

***leem**-pee^ah-loh/lah.*
Límpialo/la.

***rohm**-pay-lay ayl **ahl**-mah.*
Rómpele el alma.

pahr-tay-loh/lah.
Pártelo/la.

toom-bah-loh/lah.
Túmbalo/la.

rohm-pay-lay lah **mah**-dray.
Rómpele la madre.

mah-tah-loh/lah.
Mátalo/la.

15. Beat him/her up.

  dah-lay **oo**-nah pah-**lee**-sah.
Dale una paliza.

pay-gah-loh/lah.
Pégalo/la.

dah-lay oon poo-**tah**-soh.
Dale un putazo.

16. Kick the shit out of him/her.

dah-lay **oo**-nah **boo^ay**-nah pah-tay-**ah**-dah.
Dale una buena pateada.

pah-**tay**-ah-loh/lah **doo**-roh.
Patéalo/la duro.

17. Hit him/her.

pay-gah-loh/lah.
Pégalo/la.

dah-lay **gohl**-pay.
Dale golpe.

may-tah-lay **kahn**-yah.
Métale caña.

18. Hit him/her hard in the head.

pay-gah-loh/lah **doo**-roh ayn lah kah-**bay**-sah.
Pégalo/la duro en la cabeza.

19. Stab him/her.

nah-**bah**-hah-loh/lah.
Navájalo/la.

20. Shoot him/her.

tee-rah-loh/lah.
Tíralo/la.

foh-goh-**nay**-ah-loh/lah.
Fogonéalo/la.

dee-**spah**-rah-lo/la.
Dispáralo/la.

21. Blow his/her head off.

  boo^ay-lah-lay lah kah-**bay**-sah.
Vuélale la cabeza.

dee-**spah**-rah-lay oon cheen-**gah**-soh.
Dispárale un chingazo.

dee-**spah**-rah-lay oon trahn-**kah**-soh.
Dispárale un trancazo.

22. Get rid of it.

tee-rah-loh.
Tíralo.

*day-sah-pah-**ray**-say-loh.*
Desaparécelo.

23. Swallow it.

trah-gah-tay-loh.
Trágatelo.

24. Hide it.

*ay-**skohn**-day-loh.*
Escóndelo.

25. Keep him/her busy.

*ayn-tray-**tayn**-loh/lah.*
Entretenlo/la.

*dah-lay oon pah-**say**-oh.*
Dale un paseo.

*mahn-dah-loh/lah ah pah-say-**ahr**.*
Mándalo/la a pasear.

26. You grab him/her high, I'll grab him/her low.

*too loh/lah **koh**-hays **ahl**-toh ee yoh (loh/lah **koh**-hoh) **bah**-hoh.*
Tú lo/la cojes alto y yo (lo/la) cojo bajo.

27. He/she looks like a dumbass.

*say bay moo^ee payn-**day**-hoh/hah.*
Se ve muy pendejo/a.

*pah-**ray**-say bee^ayn payn-**day**-hoh/hah.*
Parece bien pendejo/a.

*pah-**ray**-say boo^ay.*
Parece buey.

*say bay **tohn**-toh/tah.*
Se ve tonto/a.

*say bay ee-**dee^oh**-tah.*
Se ve idiota.

28. Bust his/her mouth open.

*rray-**bee^ayn**-tah-lay lah **boh**-kah.*
Reviéntale la boca.

29. Bust his/her head wide open.

*pahr-tay-lay lah kah-**bay**-sah.*
Pártele la cabeza.

30. Give it to him/her good when he/she turns around.

*dah-say-loh bee^ayn **koo^ahn**-doh say **bee**-ray.*
Dáselo bien cuando se vire.

31. We'll grab him/her when he/she

turns around.

*see say bohl-**tay**-ah loh/lah*
Si se voltea, lo/la

*koh-**hay**-mohs.*
cojemos.

32. We'll fuck him/her up when

he/she goes to sleep.

*see say **doo^ayr**-may*
Si se duerme,

*loh/lah hoh-**day**-mohs.*
lo/la jodemos.

33. Send him/her to hell.

***mahn**-dah-loh/lah ahl kah-**rah**-hoh/een-**fee^ayr**-noh.*
Mándalo/la al carajo/infierno.

Notes

[1] This section has been provided strictly for informative purposes and to help you protect yourself. Listening to these phrases on the CD provided and pronouncing them will help you become familiar enough with them to recognize them when used.

[2] Throughout this text, the use of *le* has been incorporated to make reference to both a *male* and *female* easier for you, the speaker. However, the forms *lo (male)* and *la (female)* are provided here since native speakers will make such a distinction in speech. It is important to note such a difference should you be the target of these phrases.

Dirty Words and Insults[1,2]

Phrases

English	Pronunciation & Spanish
1. Kiss my ass.	*bay-sah-may ayl **koo**-loh.* Bésame el culo.
2. Go fuck yourself.	***cheen**-gah-tay.* Chíngate.
3. Eat shit.	*koh-may **mee^ayr**-dah.* Come mierda.
4. Suck my dick.	***mah**-mah-may lah **bayr**-gah.* Mámame la verga.
5. Go to hell.	***bay**-tay ah lah cheen-**gah**-dah.* Vete a la chingada.
6. Son of a bitch.	*ee-hoh day **poo**-tah.* Hijo de puta.
7. I shit on your mother.	*may **kah**-goh ayn too **mah**-dray.* Me cago en tu madre.
8. dumbass	*boo^ay* buey
9. bastard	*kah-**brohn**/ -nah* cabrón/a
10. liar	*aym-boo-**stay**-roh/rah* embustero/a *mayn-tee-**roh**-soh/sah* mentiroso/a
11. chicken shit/coward	*koh-**bahr**-day* cobarde
12. queer	*mah-ree-**kohn*** maricón
13. faggot	***hoh**-toh* joto
14. shit	***mee^ayr**-dah* mierda
15. asshole	*payn-**day**-hoh/hah* pendejo/a
16. whore	*rrah-**may**-rah* ramera

17. dyke	*tohr-tee-**yay**-rah* **tortillera**
18. stool pigeon/snitch	*soh-**plohn**/ -nah* **soplón/a**
19. red neck/trashy person	***nah**-koh* **naco**
20. Fuck you.	***hoh**-day-tay.* **Jódete.**
21. You're/He's/She's a rookie.	*say bay noh-**bah**-toh/tah.* **Se ve novato/a.**
22. You're/He's/She's a stupidass/idiot.	*pah-**ray**-say bee^ayn payn-**day**-hoh/hah.* **Parece bien pendejo/a.**
23. Damn you/him/her.	*mahl-**dee**-toh/tah say^ah.* **Maldito/a sea.**
24. Son of a fuck/screw.	***ee**-hoh day lah cheen-**gah**-dah.* **Hijo de la chingada.**

Notes

[1] This section has been provided strictly for informative purposes and to help you protect yourself. Listening to these phrases on the CD provided and pronouncing them will help you become familiar enough with them to recognize them when used.

[2] Remember, the *–o ending* will be heard for *males* and the *–a ending* will be heard for *females*.

Weapons

Before You Begin

The Hispanic population of the U.S. experiences higher rates of firearm related violence than the total U.S. population combined. Also, Hispanics are more likely than any other racial or ethnic group to be victims of violent crimes. Homicides, including those involving a firearm, are the seventh leading cause of death among Hispanics in general and the second leading cause of death among Hispanics ages 15 to 24. Hispanics that are victims of violent crime are more likely than any other racial or ethnic group to be victims of an offender that carries a weapon.

Phrases

English	Pronunciation & Spanish
1. Do you have a (more) weapon(s)?	*tee^ay*-nay *(mahs)* **ahr**-mah(s)? ¿Tiene (más) arma(s)?
2. Show me the weapon/the weapons!	*moo^ay*-stray-may ayl **ahr**-mah/lahs **ahr**-mahs! ¡Muéstreme el arma/las armas!
3. Put down the weapon/the weapons	**bah**-hay ayl **ahr**-mah/lahs **ahr**-mahs ¡Baje el arma/las armas
(or I'll shoot)!	*(oh dee-**spah**-roh)!* (o disparo)!
4. Give me the weapon/the weapons!	**day**-may ayl **ahr**-mah/lahs **ahr**-mahs! ¡Déme el arma/las armas!
5. Kick the weapon/the weapons over to me!	pah-**tay**-ay-may ayl **ahr**-mah/lahs **ahr**-mahs! ¡Patéeme el arma/las armas!
6. weapons (firearms)	**ahr**-mahs *(day **foo^ay**-goh)* armas (de fuego)
7. (semiautomatic) gun	**ahr**-mah day **foo^ay**-goh *(say-mee-ah^oo-toh-**mah**-tee-kah)* arma de fuego (semiautomática)
8. explosives	*ayk-sploh-**see**-bohs* explosivos
9. pistol	*pee-**stoh**-lah* pistola
10. revolver	*rray-**bohl**-bayr* revólver
11. shotgun	*ay-skoh-**pay**-tah* escopeta
12. rifle	**rree**-flay rifle

13. machine gun	*ah-may-trah-yah-**doh**-rah* ametralladora
14. knife/shank	*koo-**chee**-yoh / nah-**bah**-hah* cuchillo / navaja
15. blade	***oh**-hah / koo-**chee**-yah* hoja / cuchilla
16. bomb	***bohm**-bah* bomba
17. grenade	*grah-**nah**-dah* granada
18. dagger	*poon-**yahl*** puñal
19. bio-weapon	***ahr**-mah bee^oh-**loh**-hee-kah* arma biológica
20. chemical weapon	***ahr**-mah **kee**-mee-kah* arma química
21. brass knuckles	*noo-dee-**yay**-rahs* nudilleras
22. club/night stick	*gah-**rroh**-tay* garrote
23. (rubber) bullet	***bah**-lah (day **oo**-lay/**goh**-mah)* bala (de hule/goma)
24. body armour	*ahr-mah-**doo**-rah* armadura
25. bullet proof vest	*chah-**lay**-koh ahn-tee-**bah**-lahs* chaleco antibalas
26. I don't have anything.	*noh **tayn**-goh **nah**-dah.* No tengo nada.
27. I don't have a (any) weapon(s).	*noh **tayn**-goh (neen-**goo**-nah) **ahr**-mah.* No tengo (ninguna) arma.
28. I can't.	*noh **poo^ay**-doh.* No puedo.

Practical Activities

Weapons

A) Translation

Instructions: Translate aloud into English the following mini-dialogues. You may need to reference past chapters to assist you.

mini-dialogue I

agente: ¿Tiene arma?
sospechoso/a: No, no tengo arma.
agente: Muéstreme las manos. (Officer then sees suspect drop a pistol). Patéeme el arma. (Suspect complies). Acuéstese boca abajo y no se mueva. Coopere completamente. Voy a esposarle.

mini-dialogue II

agente: ¡Baje el arma!
sospechoso/a: No puedo.
agente: ¡Baje el arma o disparo! (Suspect complies). ¿Tiene más armas?
sospechoso/a: Sí, un cuchillo.
agente: Vacíe los bolsillos. ¡Déme las armas! (Suspect complies). Arrodíllese y entrelace las manos detrás de la nuca. Voy a registrale. Coopere completamente. Voy a arrestarle.

B) Matching

Instructions: Match the Spanish word with the corresponding English word. Practice saying each one aloud in Spanish and English after you have finished and checked your work.

1. ___ arma de fuego		a. shotgun
2. ___ nudilleras		b. blade
3. ___ puñal		c. bullet proof vest
4. ___ garrote		d. rubber bullet
5. ___ armadura		e. brass knuckles
6. ___ hoja		f. club/night stick
7. ___ bala de goma		g. dagger
8. ___ ametralladora		h. body armor
9. ___ escopeta		i. firearm
10. ___ chaleco antibalas		j. machine gun

Chapter 8

Routine Traffic Situations

Traffic Stops and Violations[1]

Before You Begin

One of the biggest obstacles for Hispanic immigrants is their lack of knowledge of U.S. laws and culture. Many of these immigrants expose themselves to greater risks because they continue to drive according to the rules and regulations of their home countries. Youth that come from Mexico are accustomed to driving without a license and being permitted to drive at a much younger age than their U.S. counterparts. The language barrier also contributes to the problem. Even when provided with materials, such as state driving manuals in Spanish, a large number of Hispanics do not understand them because the translation is poorly rendered or the Spanish used is peninsular Spanish (from Spain). Taking into account that educational materials that address traffic safety should be of a family-focused nature is essential in reaching the Hispanic population. Hispanic males tend to be more receptive to educational materials that reference the protection of family and friends than those that do not.

The rare use of seat belts and child safety seats is another cultural difference since in many parts of Latin America it is either not required by law or it is not enforced. Also, in some Latin American countries, motorists who break traffic laws use *sobornos (soh-**bohr**-nohs)*, *bribes*, or *mordidas (mohr-**dee**-dahs)*, *extra fees*, to pay off the officer for the traffic violation on the spot.

Phrases

English	Pronunciation & Spanish
1. Pull over and stop.	*ah-gah-say ah oon **lah**-doh ee **pah**-ray.* Hágase a un lado y pare.
2. Pull over to the right and stop.	*ah-gah-say ahl **lah**-doh day-**ray**-choh ee **pah**-ray.* Hágase al lado derecho y pare.
3. Turn off the motor, please.	*ah-**pah**-gay ayl moh-**tohr** pohr fah-**bohr**.* Apague el motor, por favor.
4. Please stay in your vehicle and roll down	*pohr fah-**bohr** kay-day-say ayn soo bay-**ee**-koo-loh ee **bah**-hay* Por favor, quédese en su vehículo y baje
the window	*lah bayn-tah-**nee**-yay* la ventanilla
(and keep you hands on the wheel).	*(ee mahn-**tayn**-gah lahs **mah**-nohs ayn ayl boh-**lahn**-tay).* (y mantenga las manos en el volante).

5. Good morning.	*boo^ay-nohs dee-ahs.* Buenos días. [2]	

6. Good afternoon/evening.	*boo^ay-nahs tahr-days/noh-chays.* Buenas tardes/noches. [2]

7. I'm—.	*soh^ee —-.* Soy —. [3]

8. I need to see ...	*nay-say-see-toh bayr ...* Necesito ver ...

your driver's license.
soo lee-sayn-see^ah day kohn-doo-seer.
su licencia de conducir. [4]

proof of auto/vehicle registration.
proo^ay-bah day mah-tree-koo-lah-see^ohn dayl ah^oo-toh / bay-ee-koo-loh.
prueba de matriculación del auto/vehículo.

proof of auto/vehicle insurance.
proo^ay-bah day say-goo-roh dayl ah^oo-toh / bay-ee-koo-loh.
prueba de seguro del auto/vehículo..

proof you own the vehicle.
proo^ay-bah day proh-pee^ay-dahd dayl bay-ee-koo-loh.
prueba de propiedad del vehículo.

some (photo) I.D..
ahl-goo-nah fohr-mah day ee-dayn-tee-fee-kah-see^ohn (kohn foh-toh).
alguna forma de identificación (con foto).

9. Is all of this information correct?	*ays koh-rrayk-tah toh-dah ay-stah een-fohr-mah-see^ohn?* ¿Es correcta toda esta información?

10. This has expired.	*ay-stoh say ah bayn-see-doh.* Esto se ha vencido.

11. Do you know why I've stopped you?	*sah-bah pohr kay lay pah-ray?* ¿Sabe por qué le paré?

12. Do you know how fast your were driving?	*sah-bay loh rrah-pee-doh kay kohn-doo-see-ah?* ¿Sabe lo rápido que conducía? [6]

13. The maximum/minimum speed limit is —.	*lah bay-loh-see-dahd mahk-see-mah/mee-nee-mah ays —-.* La velocidad máxima/mínima es —. [5]

14. You were driving—miles an hour.	*kohn-doo-see-ah ah—mee-yahs lah oh-rah.* Conducía a—millas la hora. [5,6]

15. You have broken the law.	*ah kay-brahn-tah-dah lah lay^ee.* Ha quebrantado la ley.

16. You have committed a moving violation.	*ah koh-may-tee-doh oo-nah een-frahk-see^ohn day trahn-see-toh* Ha cometido una infracción de tránsito

ayn oon bay-ee-koo-loh ayn mahr-chah.
en un vehículo en marcha.

17. You didn't ...

noh ...
No ...

    stop (at the light/the stop sign).

*pah-**roh**/say day-**too**-boh (**pah**-rah ayl say-**mah**-foh-roh/lay sayn-**yahl***
paró/se detuvo (para el semáforo/la señal

*day ay-**stohp**).*
de stop).

    yield (to pedestrians).

*say-dee-**oh** ayl **pah**-soh (ah lohs pay-ah-**toh**-nays).*
cedió el paso (a los peatones).

    stop at the red light.

*rray-spay-**toh** lah loos **rroh**-hah.*
respetó la luz roja.

    observe the signal.

*ohb-sayr-**boh** lah sayn-**yahl**.*
observó la señal.

    signal.

*ee-soh sayn-**yah**-lays.*
hizo señales.

    observe the school zone.

*ohb-sayr-**boh** lah **soh**-nah ay-skoh-**lahr**.*
observó la zona escolar.

    have the right to pass.

*tay-**nee**-ah day-**ray**-choh **pah**-rah ah-day-lahn-**tahr**/rray-bah-**sahr**.*
tenía derecho para adelantar/rebasar.

    observe the street sign information.

*ohb-sayr-**boh** lah een-fohr-mah-**see^ohn** dayl lay-**tray**-roh day **trahn**-see-toh.*
observó la información del letrero de tránsito.

18. You were speeding.

*ayk-say-**dee**-ah lah bay-loh-see-**dahd** payr-mee-**tee**-dah.*
Excedía la velocidad permitida.

19. You have to slow down.

***tee^ay**-nay kay rray-doo-**seer** lah bay-loh-see-**dahd**.*
Tiene que reducir la velocidad.

20. You were driving too slow.

*kohn-doo-**see**-ah day-mah-**see^ah**-doh **layn**-toh.*
Conducía demasiado lento. [6]

21. You made

ee-soh ...
Hizo ...

    an illegal lane change.

*oon **kahm**-bee^oh day kah-**rreel** ee-lay-**gahl**.*
un cambio de carril ilegal. [7]

    an illegal ("U") turn.

***oo**-nah **boo^ayl**-tah (ayn "oo") ee-lay-**gahl**.*
una vuelta (en "U") ilegal.

22. You stopped suddenly.

*pah-**roh** day rray-**payn**-tay.*
Paró de repente.

23. You didn't come to a complete stop.

*noh pah-**roh** kohm-play-tah-**mayn**-tay.*
No paró completamente.

24. You were following too close.

*say-**ghee**-ah moo^ee day **sayr**-kah.*
Seguía muy de cerca.

25. You almost had an accident.

***kah**-see **too**-boh oon ahk-see-**dayn**-tay.*
Casi tuvo un accidente.

26. You were racing.	*ah-**see**-ah kah-**rray**-rahs.* Hacía carreras.
27. Your visibility is obstructed.	*tee^**ay**-nay lah bee-see-bee-lee-**dahd** ohb-**stroo^ee**-dah.* Tiene la visibilidad obstruida.
28. You were driving recklessly.	*kohn-doo-**see**-ah kohn eem-proo-**dayn**-see^ah.* Conducía con imprudencia. [6]
29. You were weaving/swerving.	*seeg-sah-**gay^ah**-bah.* Zigzagueaba.
31. You were backing up/driving in reverse.	*ee-bah ayn **mahr**-chah ah-**trahs**.* Iba en marcha atrás.
32. You were passing/moving forward (carelessly).	*ah-day-lahn-**tah**-bah (kohn eem-proo-**dayn**-see^ah).* Adelantaba (con imprudencia).
33. You were driving in the HOV/MOV/carpool/diamond lane.	*kohn-doo-**see**-ah ayn ayl* Conducía en el *kah-**rreel pah**-rah bay-ee-koo-lohs kohn mahs day **oo**-nah payr-**soh**-nah.* carril para vehículos con más de una persona. [6]
34. You were blocking traffic.	*ohb-stroo-**ee**-ah ayl **pah**-soh.* Obstruía el paso.
35. You cannot tow/pull another vehicle (like that).	*noh **poo^ay**-day rray-mohl-**kahr oh**-troh bay-**ee**-koo-loh* No puede remolcar otro vehículo *(ah-**see**).* (así).
36. You have committed a traffic violation.	*ah koh-may-**tee**-doh **oo**-nah een-frahk-**see^ohn** day **trahn**-see-toh.* Ha cometido una infracción de tránsito.
37. Your tail lights are not working.	*lahs **loo**-says trah-**say**-rahs noh ay-**stahn** foon-see^oh-**nahn**-doh.* Las luces traseras no están funcionando.
38. Your brake lights are not working.	*lahs **loo**-says day **fray**-noh noh ay-**stahn** foon-see^oh-**nahn**-doh.* Las luces de freno no están funcionando.
39. Your turn signals are not working.	*lahs **loo**-says een-tayr-mee-**tayn**-tays noh ay-**stahn** foon-see^oh-**nahn**-doh.* Las luces intermitentes no están funcionando.
40. There are too many passengers.	*ah^ee day-mah-**see^ah**-dohs pah-say-**hay**-rohs.* Hay demasiados pasajeros.
41. You are not/He is not/She is not ... wearing a seatbelt. in a car seat.	*noh ...* No ... *yay-bah ayl seen-too-**rohn** day say-goo-ree-**dahd**.* lleva el cinturón de seguridad. *ay-**stah** ayn oon ah-**see^ayn**-toh day **kah**-rroh **pah**-rah **neen**-yohs.* está en un asiento de carro para niños.

42. You were littering.

*tee-**rah**-bah bah-**soo**-rah.*
Tiraba basura.

43. The load is not tied down properly.

*noh say ah soo-hay-**tah**-doh lah **kahr**-gah koh-rrayk-tah-**mayn**-tay.*
No se ha sujetado la carga correctamente.

44. You are hauling too much.

*ay-**stah** trahns-pohr-**tahn**-doh day-mah-**see^ah**-doh.*
Está transportando demasiado.

45. Your vehicle does not have plates.

*ayl bay-**ee**-koo-loh noh **tee^ay**-nay **plah**-kahs/mah-**tree**-koo-lah.*
El vehículo no tiene placas/matrícula.

46. The inspection sticker has expired.

*say lay ah bayn-**see**-doh lah een-spayk-**see^ohn** dayl bay-**ee**-koo-loh.*
Se le ha vencido la inspección del vehículo.

47. Your vehicle is parked in a ...

*ayl bay-**ee**-koo-loh ay-**stah** ay-stah-see^oh-**nah**-doh ayn ...*
El vehículo está estacionado en ...

    no parking zone.

*oo-nah **soh**-nah day noh ay-stah-see^oh-**nahr**.*
una zona de no estacionar.

    (passenger) loading and unloading zone.

*oo-nah **soh**-nah day **kahr**-gah ee days-**kahr**-gah (day pah-say-**hay**-rohs).*
una zona de carga y descarga (de pasajeros).

    the emergency vehicle lane.

*ayl kah-**rreel** day ay-mayr-**hayn**-see^ah.*
el carril de emergencia.

    a reserved space.

*oon ay-**spah**-see^oh rray-sayr-**bah**-doh.*
un espacio reservado.

48. It's illegal ...

*ays ee-lay-**gahl** ...*
Es ilegal ...

    to hitchhike.

*pay-**deer** ah-bayn-**tohn**.*
pedir aventón. [8]

    to park here (without permission).

*ay-stah-see^oh-**nahr** ah-**kee** (seen payr-**mee**-soh).*
estacionar aquí (sin permiso).

    to park here

*ay-stah-see^oh-**nahr** ah-**kee***
estacionar aquí

    (without a parking sticker/hang tag).

*(seen payr-**mee**-soh day ay-stah-see^oh-**nahr**).*
(sin permiso de estacionar).

49. You must pay the meter.

*tee^ay**-nay kay pah-**gahr** ayl pahr-**kee**-may-troh.*
Tiene que pagar el parquímetro.

50. You have parked illegally.

*ah ay-stah-see^oh-**nah**-doh ee-lay-gahl-**mayn**-tay.*
Ha estacionado ilegalmente.

51. I'm going to give you a ticket/warning

*lay boh^ee ah dahr **oo**-nah **mool**-tah/oon ah-**bee**-soh*
Le voy a dar una multa/un aviso

    (this time).

*(**ay**-stah bays).*
(esta vez).

yah-may ah **ay**-stay **noo**-may-roh (ah-**kee**) …

52. Call this number (here) …   Llame a este número (aquí) …

pah-rah mahs een-fohr-mah-**see^ohn**.

    for more information.   para más información.

see **tee^ay**-nay pray-**goon**-tahs.

    if you have questions.   si tiene preguntas.

pah-rah pah-**gahr** lah **mool**-tah.

    to pay the fine.   para pagar la multa.

see noh kohm-**prayn**-day.

    if you don't understand.   si no comprende.

pah-rah lah **fay**-chah day ah^oo-dee-**ayn**-see^ah.

    for the date of your hearing.   para la fecha de audiencia.

nay-say-see-tah-**rah** bay-**neer** kohn-**mee**-goh ee

53. You will need to come with me and   Necesitará venir conmigo y

day-**hahr** ayl bay-**ee**-koo-loh ah-**kee**.

    leave the vehicle here.   dejar el vehículo aquí.

pohr fah-**bohr** see^ay-rray kohn **yah**-bay ee ah-say-**goo**-ray ayl bay-**ee**-koo-loh.

54. Please lock up and secure the vehicle.   Por favor, cierre con llave y asegure el vehículo.

may nay-say-**see**-tah dahr lahs **yah**-bays.

55. You need to give me the keys.   Me necesita dar las llaves.

kay **tayn**-gah mahs koo^ee-**dah**-doh ayn ayl foo-**too**-roh.

56. Be more careful in the future.   Que tenga más cuidado en el futuro.

tee^ay-nay kay ah-**sayr** ahl-goh soh-bray **ay**-stoh

57. You have to do something about that   Tiene que hacer algo sobre eso

(**ahn**-tays day poh-**nayr** ayl bay-**ee**-koo-loh ayn **mahr**-chah).

    (before moving the vehicle).   (antes de poner el vehículo en marcha).

noh ays proo-**dayn**-tay mah-nay-**hahr** ayl bay-**ee**-koo-loh ah-**see**.

58. It is not safe to drive the vehicle like that.   No es prudente manejar el vehículo así.

Notes

[1] Also reference *Chapter 6 - Drug/Alcohol Inquiries and Procedures* for additional useful phrases.

[2] You may include *señor, señora* or *señorita*.

[3] Use the appropriate job title from *Chapter 1- Identifying Yourself and Preliminary Scene Assessment*.

[4] Remember, *manejar (mah-nay-**hahr**)* is also commonly used.

[5] Use the appropriate number from *Chapter 14 - The Basics - Numbers*.

[6] You may also use *manejaba (mah-nay-**hah**-bah)* instead of *conducía*.

[7] The word *senda (**sayn**-dah)* can also mean *lane*.

[8] The expression *hace dedo (**ah**-say **day**-doh)* is commonly used as well.

Practical Activities

Traffic Stops and Violations

A) Oral Practice

Instructions: Choose two of the four situations below and prepare the instructions indicated for those respective situations. After you have practiced them, find a partner and present both sets of instuctions. As your partner listens, (s)he should make notes that you will use to check his/her comprehension when you have finished your presentations.

Situation 1

Announce to a vehicle to pull over and stop. After you walk up to the window, greet the driver and introduce yourself. Ask for a driver's license, proof of insurance and registration. Tell the driver the maximum speed limit (make it up or write it down) and then state how many miles an hour he/she was driving. Tell the driver he/she was speeding and must slow down. State this time you will give a warning but to be more careful in the future.

Situation 2

Announce to a vehicle to pull over to the right and stop. After you walk up to the window, greet the driver and introduce yourself. Ask for a driver's license, proof of ownership and another photo I.D. Ask the driver if he/she knows why you stopped the vehicle? (response is "no"). State he/she made an illegal "U" turn and was driving recklessly. Also, you notice a male child is not in a car seat; address this issue. State you are going to give a ticket and if the driver has any questions he/she can call this number (make it up or write it down) for more information or if he/she doesn't understand.

Situation 3

After stopping a vehicle you see the driver is starting to get out of the car. Tell him/her to turn off the car, stay inside, roll down the window and keep his/her hands on the wheel where you can see them. You then ask for a driver's license and noticed is has expired. Tell the driver he/she was racing and almost had an accident. Also, tell him/her he/she has broken the law. Instruct the driver to come with you and leave the vehicle where it is, but first lock and secure it.

Situation 4

Greet the driver of a stopped car and introduce yourself. Tell the driver the vehicle's brake lights are not working and that he/she has parked in a passenger loading and unloading zone, which is not allowed. You also notice the load the vehicle is carrying is not properly tied down and is too heavy. Instruct the driver to do something about the problem before moving the vehicle since it is not safe to drive it like that. Let the driver know you are giving him/her a warning.

B) Singular and Plural

Instructions: Sometimes it may be important to be more specific when giving information. For example, telling a motorist *the brake lights are not working* is obviously only useful if both brake lights are not working.

Therefore, the importance of knowing how to manipulate a few of the phrases from this section is rather useful. Take a look at the following example:

Phrase # 36 reads:

Your tail lights are not working. / Las luces traseras no están funcionando.

(The bolded letters in the Spanish phrase indicate the plural form.)

The phrase above is obviously talking about *both tail lights*. However, consider the same phrase when *one tail light* is out:

Your tail light is not working. / La luz trasera no está funcionando.

(The bolded letters in Spanish are lost - La~~s~~ luz~~ees~~ trasera~~s~~ no está~~n~~ funcionando.)

You may notice the word *luces* becomes *luz*. Don't worry about why, just remember it sounds the same but without the *-es*. Also, this word is an exceptional case. Likewise, it is equally important to let the motorist know which light is out: left or right. In which case, you learned in *Chapter 3* that the description comes after the noun. Remember, *right (derecho) arm (brazo)* in Spanish is *brazo derecho* not *derecho brazo*. Here, the focus in on the *tail light (luz trasera)*. Notice *trasera* ends with an *-a*, so you must choose the form of *derecho/a* or *izquierdo/a* that ends with an *-a*. Study the following examples:

the right tail light/la luz trasera derecha   the left tail light/la luz trasera izquierda

Now look at the phrase "*Your right tail light is not working*" in Spanish.

La luz trasera derecha no está funcionando.

Talk with a classmate or as a class, about how the sentence was manipulated to come up with this structure. After everyone is clear on the explanations, attempt to translate the following phrases into Spanish, in pairs, in groups or as a class. Space has been provided for you if you wish to write them out. When finished, practice saying the new expressions aloud. Also, comment on the ways in which the original phrases were manipulated to achieve the new expressions.

1. Your brake lights are not working. (original phrase from text #37)

2. Your right brake light is not working.

3. Your left brake light is not working.

4. Your turn signals are not working. (original phrase from text #38)

5. Your left turn signal is not working.

6. Your right turn signal is not working.

Driving While Impaired/Under the Influence[1]

Before You Begin

Many studies indicate that Hispanic men are at a higher risk of being involved in a traffic accident involving alcohol more so than non-Hispanics. Also, it is not uncommon to find many illegal immigrants driving vehicles with false plates that are registered to other persons. Therefore, when a crash occurs and such an individual is involved, he/she typically flees the site before police arrive. Likewise, illegal immigrants are likely to carry fake identification or invalid driver's licenses in which case a written ticket is useless. In the case that a court appearance is required, many will fail to show up.

Phrases

English	Pronunciation & Spanish
1. Pull over and stop.	*ah-gah-say ah oon lah-doh ee pah-ray.* Hágase a un lado y pare.
2. Pull over to the right and stop.	*ah-gah-say ahl lah-doh day-ray-choh ee pah-ray.* Hágase al lado derecho y pare.
3. Turn off the motor, please.	*ah-pah-gay ayl moh-tohr pohr fah-bohr.* Apague el motor, por favor.
4. Please stay in your vehicle and roll down	*pohr fah-bohr kay-day-say ayn soo bay-ee-koo-loh ee bah-hay* Por favor, quédese en su vehículo y baje
the window (and put/keep	*lah bayn-tah-nee-yay (ee pohn-gah/mahn-tayn-gah* la ventanilla (y ponga/mantenga
you hands on the wheel).	*lahs mah-nohs ayn ayl boh-lahn-tay).* las manos en el volante).
5. Good morning.	*boo^ay-nohs dee-ahs.* Buenos días.[2]
6. Good afternoon/evening.	*boo^ay-nahs tahr-days/noh-chays.* Buenas tardes/noches.[2]
7. I'm—.	*soh^ee—.* Soy—.[3]
8. I need to see ...	*nay-say-see-toh bayr ...* Necesito ver ...
your driver's license.	*soo lee-sayn-see^ah day kohn-doo-seer.* su licencia de conducir.[4]
proof of auto/vehicle registration.	*proo^ay-bah day mah-tree-koo-lah-see^ohn dayl ah^oo-toh/bay-ee-koo-loh.* prueba de matriculación del auto/vehículo.
proof of auto/vehicle insurance.	*proo^ay-bah day say-goo-roh dayl ah^oo-toh/bay-ee-koo-loh.* prueba de seguro del auto/vehículo.

proof you own the vehicle.	*proo^ay-bah day proh-pee^ay-**dahd** dayl bay-**ee**-koo-loh.* prueba de propiedad del vehículo.
some (photo) I.D..	*ahl-**goo**-nah **fohr**-mah de ee-dayn-tee-fee-kah-**see^ohn** (kohn **foh**-toh).* alguna forma de identificación (con foto).

9. Is all of this information correct?	*ays koh-**rrayk**-tah **toh**-dah **ay**-stah een-fohr-mah-**see^ohn**?* ¿Es correcta toda esta información?

10. This has expired.	***ay**-stoh say ah bayn-**see**-doh.* Esto se ha vencido.

11. Do you know why I've stopped you?	***sah**-bay pohr kay lay pah-**ray**?* ¿Sabe por qué le paré?

12. You were weaving/swerving.	*ay-**stah**-bah seeg-sah-**gay^ahn**-doh.* Estaba zigzagueando.

13. Have you been drinking?	*ah ay-**stah**-doh toh-**mahn**-doh?* ¿Ha estado tomando?

14. Did you drink ...	*toh-**moh** …* ¿Tomó …
beer?	*sayr-**bay**-sah?* cerveza?
wine?	***bee**-noh?* vino?
liquor?	*lee-**kohr** foo^ayr-tay?* licor fuerte?
something else?	***ahl**-goh mahs?* algo más?

15. How many drinks did you have?	*koo^**ahn**-tahs bay-**bee**-dahs ahl-koh-oh-lee-kahs ah toh-**mah**-doh?* ¿Cuántas bebidas alcohólicas ha tomado?

16. Did you have your last drink	*ah-say mahs/**may**-nohs day **oo**-nah **oh**-rah* ¿Hace más/menos de una hora
more/less than an hour ago?	*kay toh-**moh** soo **ool**-tee-mah bay-**bee**-dah ahl-koh-**oh**-lee-kah?* que tomó su última bebida alcohólica?

17. Are you drunk?	*ay-**stah** boh-**rrah**-choh/chah?* ¿Está borracho/a? [5]

18. What do you have ...	*kay **tee^ay**-nay …* ¿Qué tiene …
on the seat?	*ayn-**see**-mah dayl ah-**see^ayn**-toh?* encima del asiento?
under the seat?	*day-**bah**-hoh dayl ah-**see^ayn**-toh?* debajo del asiento?

behind the seat?	*day-**trahs** dayl ah-**see**^ayn-toh?* detrás del asiento?
in the back?	*ayn lah **pahr**-tay trah-**say**-rah?* en la parte trasera?
in the floorboard?	*ayn ayl **pee**-soh dayl bay-**ee**-koo-loh?* en el piso del vehículo?
in the glovebox?	*ayn lah goo^ahn-**tay**-rah?* en la guantera?
in the cup?	*ayn ayl **bah**-soh?* en el vaso?
in the bag?	*ayn lah **bohl**-sah?* en la bolsa?
in the bottle?	*ayn lah boh-**tay**-yah?* en la botella?
in the container?	*ayn ayl rray-see-**pee**^ayn-tay/ayl ayn-**bah**-say?* en el recipiente/el envase?

19. Are you hiding anything in the car?	*ay-**stah** ay-skohn-**dee**^ayn-doh **ahl**-goh ayn ayl bay-**ee**-koo-loh?* ¿Está escondiendo algo en el vehículo? [6]

20. Please step out of the vehicle and keep	*pohr fah-**bohr** **bah**-hay-say dayl bay-**ee**-koo-loh ee mahn-**tayn**-gah* Por favor, bájese del véhículo y mantenga
your hands where I can see them.	*lahs **mah**-nohs **dohn**-day lahs **poo**^ay-doh bayr.* las manos donde las puedo ver.

21. Please cooperate fully.	*pohr fah-**bohr** koh-oh-**pay**-ray kohm-play-tah-**mayn**-tay.* Por favor, coopere completamente.

22. I am not going to do you any harm.	*noh lay boh^ee ah ah-**sayr** neen-**goon dahn**-yoh.* No le voy a hacer ningún daño.

23. This is standard procedure.	***ay**-stoh ays ayl proh-toh-**koh**-loh nohr-**mahl**.* Esto es el protocolo normal.

24. It is illegal to ...	*ays ee-lay-**gahl** ...* Es ilegal ...
drink and drive.	*toh-**mahr** ahl-koh-**ohl** ee kohn-doo-**seer**.* tomar alcohol y conducir. [4]
consume alcohol as a minor	*kohn-soo-**meer** ahl-koh-**ohl** **koh**-moh oon may-**nohr** day ay-**dahd*** consumir alcohol como un menor de edad
(youger than twenty-one years of age).	*may-**nohs** day bay^een-tee-**oon** **ahn**-yohs day ay-**dahd**).* (menos de veintiún años de edad).
buy alcohol for a minor.	*kohm-**prahr** ahl-koh-**ohl** **pah**-rah oon may-**nohr** day ay-**dahd**.* comprar alcohol para un menor de edad.

buy alcohol as a minor.	*kohm-**prahr** ahl-koh-**ohl** **koh**-moh oon may-**nohr** day ay-**dahd** comprar alcohol como un menor de edad.
to have an open container	*tay-**nayr** oon rray-see-**pee^ayn**-tay/oon ayn-**bah**-say day ahl-koh-**ohl*** tener un recipiente/un envase de alcohol
in a vehicle.	*ah-**bee^ayr**-toh ayn oon bay-ee-koo-loh.* abierto en un vehículo.
to drink in public.	*toh-**mahr** ayn **poo**-blee-koh.* tomar en público.
25. Where did you buy this?	***dohn**-day kohm-**proh** ay-stoh?* ¿Dónde compró esto?
26. Who bought it for you?	*kee^ayn say loh kohm-**proh**?* ¿Quién se lo compró?
27. I am going to carry you to a detention facility	*boh^ee ah yay-**bahr**-lay ah oon **sayn**-troh day day-tayn-**see^ohn*** Voy a llevarle a un centro de detención
(until we can contact a legal	*(**ah**-stah kay poh-**dah**-mohs koh-moo-nee-**kahr**-nohs kohn oon too-**tohr*** (hasta que podamos comunicarnos con un tutor
guardian).	*lay-**gahl**).* legal).
28. Please calm down and follow my instructions.	*pohr fah-**bohr kahl**-may-say ee **see**-gah mees een-strook-**see^oh**-nays.* Por favor, cálmese y siga mis instrucciones.

Notes

[1] Also reference *Chapter 4 - Useful Commands, Chapter 6 - Drug/Alcohol Inquiries and Procedures, Chapter 8 - Routine Traffic Stops, Chapter 9 - Miranda Rights,* and *Chapter 11 - Criminal Activity* for additional phrases and expressions. If you need to speak directly to a minor/juvenile, consult Chapter 11 – Criminal Activity – Dealing with Juveniles/Minors.

[2] You may include *señor, señora* or *señorita.*

[3] Use the appropriate job title from *Chapter 1 - Identifying Yourself and Preliminary Scene Assessment.*

[4] Once again, *conducir* and *manejar (mah-nay-**hahr**)* are interchangeable.

[5] Use *-o* with *males* and *-a* with *females.*

[6] See *Chapter 16 - Expressing the Location of People, Places and Things.*

Practical Activities

Driving While Impaired/Under the Influence

A) Oral Practice

Instructions: Read and assess the following scenarios and decide what you would say to or ask the motorist. Include at least *one statement* and *one question* for each one.

Example: *You stop a motorist who is swerving.*

You might say and/or ask – *Estaba zigzagueando. ¿Ha estado tomando?*

1. The smell of alcohol is coming from the interior of a motorist's vehicle.
2. You ask for I.D. and verify the information only to find out it has expired.
3. A small brown paper bag is partially hidden under the passenger seat.
4. The motorist appears to have had something to drink before getting in the vehicle.
5. A passenger is acting suspicious and keeps glancing at an open drink container.
6. At a routine traffic stop, the driver of the vehicle seems very nervous.
7. You suspect a passenger for obtaining alcohol for a minor in the car.
8. Outside a bar, a patron is rowdy and boisterous.

B) Translation

Instructions: In pairs, translate the following dialogue into English. After you have finished, find another pair and check your translation against theirs. Try not to look back at this section or any other chapter before you have attempted the entire translation and consulted with another pair. Finally, to resolve any discrepancies, consult the text and make the necessary corrections. If time permits, practice the dialogue with a classmate, each one taking turns in both roles.

agente: Apague el motor, por favor. Quédese en su vehículo y ponga las manos en el volante. Soy——-. Necesito ver su licencia de conducir, prueba de seguro del vehículo y prueba de matriculación del vehículo, por favor.

motorista: Sí, como no.

agente: ¿Sabe por qué le paró?

motorista: Lo siento, no señor.

agente: Estaba zigzagueando y adelantaba sin prudencia. ¿Ha estado tomando?

motorista: Un poco, señor.

agente: ¿Tomó cerveza o licor fuerte?

motorista: Sólo cerveza.

agente: ¿Cuántas bebidas alcohólicas ha tomado?

motorista: No sé ... tres.

agente: ¿Hace más o menos de una hora que tomó su última bebida?

motorista: Más de una hora, sí.

agente: ¿Qué tiene en el envase?

motorist: Nada.

agente: Por favor, bájese del vehículo y mantenga las manos donde las puedo ver. No le voy a hacer ningún daño. Esto es el protocolo normal. Voy a registrarle. Separe las piernas y coopere completamente. Es ilegal tomar alcohol y conducir y tener un envase de alcohol abierto en el vehículo. Voy a llevarle a un centro de detención. Por favor, cierre con llave y asegure el vehículo.

Cyber-Investigation

What information can you find on the internet that explains the possible reasons for alcohol abuse and/or substance abuse among Hispanics? How does this general information vary when considering a person's socieconomic status, immigration status, morals and values? Lastly, why is there a demographic variation in this information?

Administering an Alcohol Test/Breathalyzer[1]

Before You Begin

In a research study, it was found that Hispanic drivers are more likely to consume more alcohol, more frequently than Anglo drivers. It also showed that they are more likely to drive with a blood alcohol concentration (BAC) level over .05 percent. The same study concluded that Hispanics believe it takes six to eight drinks to impact one's ability to operate a vehicle, while Anglos responded that it takes only two to four. Regarding teens and alcohol consumption, Hispanic male teens are two times as likely to die in a car crash than their Anglo counterparts. Notably, the vast majority of the Hispanic community does not condone driving while impaired and actually considers it socially unacceptable.

Phrases

English	Pronunciation & Spanish
1. I am going to give you a …	*lay boh^ee ah dahr* **oo**-*nah …* Le voy a dar una …
field sobriety test.	**proo^ay**-*bah day soh-bree^ay*-**dahd** *ayn ayl* **see**-*tee^oh.* prueba de sobriedad en el sitio.
urine test.	**proo^ay**-*bah day oh*-**ree**-*nah.* prueba de orina.[2]
a breathalyzer test.	**proo^ay**-*bah day ahl-koh*-**lee**-*may-troh.* prueba de alcoholímetro.
2. If you refuse to take the test,	*see rray*-**chah**-*sah soh-may*-**tayr**-*say ah lah* **proo^ay**-*bah* Si rechaza someterse a la prueba,
you may lose your license.	**poo^ay**-*day kay rray*-**boh**-*kayn soo lee*-**sayn**-*see^ay.* puede que revoquen su licencia.
3. It's the law and you must obey.	*ays lah lay^ee ee* **tee^ay**-*nay kay koom*-**pleer** *kohn* **ay**-*yah.* Es la ley y tiene que cumplir con ella.
4. If not, I will have to arrest you and	*see noh tayn*-**dray** *kay ah-rray*-**stahr**-*lay ee* Si no, tendré que arrestarle y
take you to jail.	*yay*-**bahr**-*lay ah lah* **kahr**-*sayl.* llevarle a la cárcel.
5. It's your choice.	*ays soo ay-layk*-**see^ohn.** Es su elección.
6. You will need to do exactly what I say.	*nay-say-***see**-*tah ah*-**sayr** *ayk-sahk-tah-***mayn**-*tay loh kay yoh* **dee**-*goh .* Necesita hacer exactamente lo que yo digo.
7. Follow the object I show you	**see**-*gah ayl ohb*-**hay**-*toh kay lay* **moo^ay**-*stro* Siga el objeto que le muestro
only with your eyes.	**soh**-*loh kohn lohs* **oh**-*hohs.* sólo con los ojos.

8. Don't move your head.	*noh **moo^ay**-bah lah kah-**bah**-sah.* No mueva la cabeza.
9. Raise your right/left leg	*lay-**bahn**-tay lah **pee^ayr**-nah day-**ray**-chah/ees-**kee^ayr**-dah* Levante la pierna derecha/izquierda
with your arms by your side.	*ee payr-mah-**nays**-kah day **pee^ay** kohn lohs **brah**-sohs ah soo **lah**-doh.* y permanezca de pie con los brazos a su lado.
10. Count slowly from 1 to 30.	*koo^**ayn**-tay layn-tah-**mayn**-tay day **oo**-noh **ah**-stah **tray^een**-tah.* Cuente lentamente de uno hasta treinta. [3]
11. Stand here	*pohn-gah-say ah-**kee*** Póngase aquí
(on this line and put your feet together).	*(ayn **ay**-stah **lee**-nay-ah ee **pohn**-gah lohs pee^ays **hoon**-tohs).* (en esta línea y ponga los pies juntos).
12. Walk this line heel-to-toe	*kah-**mee**-nay ayn **ay**-stah **lee**-nay-ah kohn ayl tah-**lohn** day oon **pee^ay*** Camine en esta línea con el talón de un pie
	*kohn-trah lah **poon**-tah day **oh**-troh* contra la punta de otro
(until I tell you to stop).	*(**ah**-stah kay lay **dee**-gah kay **pah**-ray).* (hasta que le diga que pare).
13. Turn around and walk back	*day **oo**-nah **may**-dee^ah **boo^ayl**-tah ee **see**-gah kah-mee-**nahn**-doh* Dé una media vuelta y siga caminando
in the same manner.	*day lah **mees**-mah mah-**nay**-rah.* de la misma manera.
14. Stop.	***pah**-ray.* Pare.
15. Touch your nose with	***toh**-kay lah nah-**rees** kohn* Toque la nariz con
your right/left index finger.	*ayl **day**-doh **een**-dee-say day-**ray**-choh/ees-**kee^ayr**-doh.* el dedo índice derecho/izquierdo.[3]
16. Now do whatever I do.	*ah-**oh**-rah **ah**-gah loh kay **ah**-gah yoh.* Ahora, haga lo que haga yo.
17. Place this between your lips.	***pohn**-gah **ay**-stoh **ayn**-tray lohs **lah**-bee^ohs.* Ponga esto entre los labios.
18. Take a deep breath and blow.	*rray-**spee**-ray **ohn**-doh ee **soh**-play.* Respire hondo y sople.
19. You need to do it again.	*nay-say-**see**-tah ah-**sayr**-loh **oh**-trah bays.* Necesita hacerlo otra vez.
20. Wait here.	*ay-**spay**-ray ah-**kee**.* Espere aquí.

21. I am arrresting you for driving under

*lay ay-**stoh**^ee ah-rray-**stahn**-doh pohr kohn-doo-**seer** ayn*
Le estoy arrestando por conducir en

the influence/while impaired/
drunk driving.

*ay-**stah**-doh day aym-bree^ah-**gays**.*
estado de embriaguez. [5]

Notes

[1] Also reference *Chapter 4 - Useful Commands, Chapter 6 - Drug/Alcohol Inquiries and Procedures, Chapter 8 - Routine Traffic Stops* and *Chapter 9 - Miranda Rights* for additional useful phrases.

[2] See *Chapter 6 - Administering a Urine Test* for additional necessary phrases.

[3] See *Chapter 14 - The Basics - Numbers* to assist you in comprehension.

[4] See *Chapter 18 - Body Parts* for more vocabulary.

[5] The lower register expression *"conducir borracho/a" (kohn-doo-**seer** boh-**rrah**-choh/chah)* may be used in place of *"conducir en estado de embriaguez"* to simplify the reason for arrest if the driver does not appear to understand. Just remember to use the *-o ending* for *males* and the *-a ending* for *females*.

Practical Activities

Administering an Alcohol Test/Breathalyzer

A) Oral Practice

Instructions: With a partner, practice administering the following tests to detect alcohol. Have one person start out as the test administrator while the other plays the role of a person being tested. Switch roles and repeat the test before moving onto the next one. Try to vary the phrases as much as possible so that each person's test instructions are not exactly the same.

Test 1 – Administer a field sobriety test (use a minimum of 8 different phrases).

Test 2 – Administer a breathalyzer (use a minimum of 8 different phrases).

Follow-up

If time permits, present one of your tests to the class. Ask them to make notes about the what is happening as they listen and watch. Check for comprehension by asking a few questions in English about what happened during the test administration after your presentation.

B) Matching

Instructions: Match the beginning of each phrase from the first column with the correct ending from the second column. Then practice saying each phrase aloud and giving the English meaning.

1. ___ Si no, tendré que arrestarle y …   a. caminando de la misma manera.

2. ___ Siga el objeto que …   b. los labios. Respire hondo y sople.

3. ___ Dé una media vuelta y siga …   c. y permanezca de pie con los brazos a su lado.

4. ___ Ponga esto entre …   d. le muestro sólo con los ojos.

5. ___ Si rechaza someterse a …   e. elección.

6. ___ Levante la pierna derecha …   f. llevarle a la cárcel.

7. ___ Es su …   g. lo que yo digo.

8. ___ Necesita hacer exactamente …   h. la prueba, puede que revoquen su licencia.

Cyber-Investigation

Search for information, statistics, etc. that discuss the impact of alcohol on all teens. Then look for further information that breaks down this information demographically. Point out any noticeable trends and compare and contrast where Hispanics fall in these categories. Share your findings with the class. Does any of this information shock you? Why or why not?

Traffic Accidents and Calling for Emergency Assistance[1]

Before You Begin

According to a 2001 National Highway Traffic Safety Administration (NHTSA) article on promoting the use of seat belts among Hispanics, it was determined that the leading cause of death for Hispanics 24 years old and younger was motor vehicle crashes. This was also the second leading cause of death for Hispanics between 25 and 44 years of age. Statistics gathered for this article concluded that socioeconomic status and not necessarily ethnicity played a large part in these cases since traffic-related dangers are more prevalent in densely populated areas where the poverty rate is higher. Whereas traffic safety efforts tend to reach members of mainstream culture, they often fail to reach those outside of it. Reasons such as not crossing language and cultural barriers account for much of the problem with the dissemination of this information.

Phrases

English	Pronunciation & Spanish
1. I'm —.	*soh^ee —.* Soy —.[2]
2. I'm here to help (you).	*ay-stoh^ee ah-kee pah-rah ah^ee-yoo-dahr-(lay).* Estoy aquí para ayudar(le).
3. I'm going to help (you).	*boh^ee ah ah^ee-yoo-dahr-(lay).* Voy a ayudar(le).
4. Do you speak English?	*ah-blah een-glays?* ¿Habla inglés?
5. Does someone here speak English?	*ah^ee ahl-ghee^ayn ah-kee kay ah-blay een-glays?* ¿Hay alguien aquí que hable inglés?
6. Please try to remain calm.	*pohr fah-bohr payr-mah-nays-kah(n) kahl-moh(s)/mah(s).* Por favor, permanezca(n) calmo(s)/a(s). [3,4]
7. I am going to call 9 1 1	*yah-moh ahl noo^ay-bay oo-noh oo-noh* Llamo al 9 1 1
for emergency assitance.	*pah-rah pay-deer sayr-bee-see^ohs day ay-mayr-hayn-see^ah.* para pedir servicios de emergencia.
8. Do you want me to call for	*kee^ay-ray kay lay pee-dah* ¿Quiere que le pida
roadside assistance?	*sayr-bee-see^ohs day ay-see-stayn-see^ah ayn ayl kay-mee-noh?* servicios de asistencia en el camino?
9. I am going to request an interpreter.	*boh^ee ah pay-deer ah oon een-tayr-pray-tay.* Voy a pedir a un intérprete.
10. Is anyone injured?	*ahl-ghee^ayn ay-stah ay-ree-doh?* ¿Alguien está herido?

11. Remain still and don't try to move.

*ay-stay(n)-say **kee^ay**-toh(s)/tah(s) ee noh ayn-**tayn**-tay(n) moh-**bayr**-say.*
Este(n)se quieto(s)/a(s) y no intente(n) moverse. [3,4]

12. More help is on the way.

*bee^**ay**-nay mahs ah^ee-**yoo**-dah moo^ee **prohn**-toh.*
Viene más ayuda muy pronto.

13. Everyone please back away/clear out.

*pohr fah-**bohr** rray-troh-**say**-dahn/**lahr**-gayn-say.*
Por favor, retrocédan/lárguense. [5]

14. Let us through. [to a group]

*ah-brah-nohs **pah**-soh.*
Abrannos paso.

15. I can only speak to one person at a time.

*poo^**ay**-doh ah-**blahr**-lay soh-loh ah **oo**-nah payr-**soh**-nah ah lah bays.*
Puedo hablarle sólo a una persona a la vez.

16. Speak clearly and slowly, please.

*ah-blay **klah**-rah ee layn-tah-**mayn**-tay pohr fah-**bohr**.*
Hable clara y lentamente, por favor.

17. Who is the driver of this vehicle?

*kee^ayn ays ayl kohn-dook-**tohr** day **ay**-stay bay-ee-**koo**-loh?*
¿Quién es el conductor de este vehículo?

18. Whose vehicle is this?

*day kee^ayn ays ayl bay-ee-**koo**-loh?*
¿De quién es el vehículo?

19. Are you authorized to drive this vehicle?

*tee^**ay**-nay ah^oo-toh-ree-sah-**see^ohn** pah-rah mah-nay-**hahr ay**-stay bay-ee-**koo**-loh?*
¿Tiene autorización para manejar este vehículo? [6]

20. Who are the passengers?

*kee^**ay**-nays sohn lohs pah-sah-**hay**-rohs?*
¿Quiénes son los pasajeros?

21. Was everyone wearing a seatbelt?

*oo-**sah**-bah **toh**-dah payr-**soh**-nah ayl seen-too-**rohn** day say-goo-ree-**dahd**?*
¿Usaba toda persona el cinturón de seguridad?

22. I need to see ...

*nay-say-**see**-toh bayr ...*
Necesito ver ...

    your driver's license.

*soo lee-**sayn**-see^ah day kohn-doo-**seer**.*
su licencia de conducir. [6]

    proof of auto/vehicle registration.

*proo^**ay**-bah day mah-tree-koo-lah-**see^ohn** dayl ah^**oo**-toh/bay-ee-koo-loh.*
prueba de matriculación del auto/vehículo.

    proof of auto/vehicle insurance.

*proo^**ay**-bah day say-**goo**-roh dayl ah^**oo**-toh/bay-ee-koo-loh.*
prueba de seguro del auto/vehículo.

    proof you own the vehicle.

*proo^**ay**-bah day proh-pee^**ay**-dahd dayl bay-ee-koo-loh.*
prueba de propiedad del vehículo.

    some (photo) I.D..

*ahl-**goo**-nah **fohr**-mah de ee-dayn-tee-fee-kah-**see^ohn** (kohn **foh**-toh).*
alguna forma de identificación (con foto).

23. It's illegal to drive a vehicle without insurance.

*ays ee-lay-**gahl** mah-nay-**hahr** oon bay-ee-koo-loh seen say-**goo**-roh.*
Es ilegal manejar un vehículo sin seguro. [6]

24. Is all of this information correct?

*ays koh-**rrayk**-tah **toh**-dah **ay**-stah een-fohr-mah-**see^ohn**?*
¿Es correcta toda esta información?

25. Please (do not) move your vehicle (to the hard shoulder of the road).

*pohr fah-**bohr** (noh) **moo^ay**-bah(n) soo bay-**ee**-koo-loh (ahl ahr-**sayn**).*
Por favor, (no) mueva(n) su vehículo (al arcén).

26. Are there any eye-witnesses?

*ah^ee tay-**stee**-gohs oh-koo-**lah**-rays?*
Hay testigos oculares?

27. What is ...

koo-ahl ays ...
¿Cuál es ...

your name?

*soo **nom**-bray?*
su nombre?

your phone number (at work)?

*soo **noo**-may-roh day tay-**lay**-foh-noh (ayn ayl trah-**bah**-hoh)?*
su número de teléfono (en el trabajo)?

your address?

*soo dee-rayk-**see^ohn**?*
su dirección?

28. Who is at fault?

*kee^ayn **tee^ay**-nay lah **kool**-pah?*
¿Quién tiene la culpa?

29. Was it a ...

***oo**-boh ...*
¿Hubo ...

blowout?

*oon rray-bayn-**tohn**?*
un reventón?

mechanical problems?

*proh-**blay**-mahs may-**kah**-nee-**kohs**?*
problemas mecánicos?

30. Was it a hit-and-run?

*foo^ay oon **choh**-kay ee **foo**-gah?*
¿Fue un choque y fuga?

31. Was it because of ...

foo^ay pohr ...
¿Fue por ...

the weather?

*ayl **tee^aym**-poh?*
el tiempo?

an animal?

*oon ah-nee-**mahl**?*
un animal?

the road condition(s)?

*lah(s) kohn-dee-**see^ohn**(-ays) day lah **kah**-yay?*
la(s) condición(es) de la calle?

a pothole?

***oo**-nah **bah**-chay?*
una bache?

a pedestrian?

*oon pay-ah-**tohn**?*
un peatón?

road debris?

*ay-**skohm**-brohs ayn lah **kah**-yay?*
escombros en la calle?

a problem with the traffic light?

*oon proh-**blay**-mah kohn ayl say-**mah**-foh-roh?*
un problema con el semáforo?

another (other) vehicle(s)?

***oh**-troh(s) bay-**ee**-koo-loh(s)?*
otro(s) vehículo(s)?

32. Did someone lose control of the vehicle?	*payr-dee-**oh** ahl-ghee^ayn ayl kohn-**trohl** dayl bay-**ee**-koo-loh?* ¿Perdió alguien el control del vehículo?
33. Did someone run the red light?	*say sayl-**toh** ahl-ghee^ayn ayl say-**mah**-foh-roh ayn **rroh**-hoh?* ¿Se saltó alguien el semáforo en rojo?
34. Who?	*kee^ayn?* ¿Quién?
35. The other driver/motorist.	*ayl **oh**-troh/lah **ot**-trah choh-**fayr**/moh-toh-**rees**-tah.* El otro/La otra chofer/motorista.[7]
36. He did/She did.	*ayl/**ay**-yah.* El/Ella.
37. They did.	***ay**-yohs/**ay**-yahs.* Ellos/Ellas.[9]
38. Show me the damage done to your vehicle.	*moo^**ay**-stray-may ayl **dahn**-yoh **ay**-choh ah soo bay-**ee**-koo-loh.* Muéstreme el daño hecho a su vehículo.
39. The drivers need to exchange	*lohs kohn-dook-**toh**-rays nay-say-**see**-tahn kahm-**bee^ahr*** Los conductores necesitan cambiar
(insurance) information	*een-fohr-mah-**see^ohn** (day say-**goo**-roh).* información (de seguro).
40. I will file a report	*boh^ee ah ay-mee-**teer** oon een-**fohr**-may* Voy a emitir un informe
(after speaking …	*(day-**spoo^ays** day ayn-tree-bee-**stahr** …* (después de entrevistar …
to all parties involved).	*ah **toh**-dahs lahs **pahr**-tays een-boh-loo-**krah**-dahs).* a todas las partes involucradas).
to all of the eye witnesses).	*ah **toh**-dohs lohs tay-**stee**-gohs oh-koo-**lah**-rays).* a todos los testigos oculares).
41. I'll call for a tow truck.	*boh^ee ah pay-**deer** oo-nah **groo**-ah/oon rray-**mohl**-kay.* Voy a pedir una grúa/un remolque.
42. (Everyone) wait here.	*ay-**spay**-ray(n) ah-**kee**.* Espere(n) aquí.[3]

Notes

[1] You may also want to use phrases from *Chapter 8: Routine Traffic Stops and Violations* to assist you in citing a driver, etc.

[2] Use the appropriate job title from *Chapter 1 - Identifying Yourself and Preliminary Scene Assessment.*

[3] The *"(n)"* in many of the commands given in this chapter indicate the possibility of a *singular form* and a *plural form*. For example, the command *"Speak"* appears as *"Hable(n)."* To tell one person *"Speak,"* use *"Hable."* If addressing two or more people use *"Hablen."*

[4] Use the *-o ending* when talking to a *male* and the *-a ending* when talking to a *female*. Likewise, if addressing a *group of males* or a *mixed group (males and females)*, use the *-os ending*. If talking to a *group of females* use the *-as ending*.

[5] The expression "*Háganse para allá*" may also be used in this situation to back spectators aways but takes on a lower register.

[6] Remember, *manejar (mah-nay-**hahr**)* is interchangeable with *conducir*.

[7] *El otro chofer/motorista* refers to a *male* and *La otra chofer/motorista* refers to a *female*.

[8] To specifically say *inclement weather,* use *intemperie (een-tam-**pay**-ree^ay)*.

[9] *Ellos* refers to a groups of *males* or a *mixed group*, whereas, *Ellas* can only refer to a group of *females*.

Practical Activities

Traffic Accidents and Calling for Emergency Assistance

A) Oral Practice

Instructions: Prepare what you will say in Spanish according to the information given in each situation. You may want to consult previous chapters as well as *Chapter 15 – Family and Friends* for additional vocabulary. After you have finished, find a partner and decide who will play the public safety official and who will be the Spanish-speaker involved in dialogue 1 and dialogue 2. Then, rehearse each dialogue according to your respective role. After approximately 10 minutes of rehearsing, form a group of 4 with another pair and present your prepared dialogues. Listeners should try to observe the reenactment without looking at the text and glean meaning from the presentation. Remember, body language can also help you improve your communication skills when speaking a foreign language.

Situation 1:
Public Safety Official

1. I'm —. I'm here to help.

2. Do you speak English?

3. Please try to remain calm. I am requesting an interpreter.

4. Is anyone hurt?

5. (Speaking to the daughter) Remain still and try not to move. More help is on the way.

6. Who is the driver of this vehicle?

7. Are you authorized to drive this vehicle?

8. Please move your vehicle to the hard shoulder of the road.

Situation 1:
Spanish-Speaker

1. Thank you.

2. A little.

3. Fine/Okay.

4. My daughter.

5. —

6. I am.

7. Yes.

8. Of course, officer.

Situation 2:
Public Safety Official

1. I'm —. I'm going to help you.

2. Everyone please move away.
   (Speaking to the victim) Remain still and try not to move.

3. Who are the passengers?

4. Was everyone wearing a seatbelt?

5. Are there any eye-witnesses?

6. (Speaking to the brother). What's your name?

7. Who is at fault?

8. Everyone wait here.

Situation 2:
Spanish-Speaker

1. Yes, please.

2. Okay.

3. My brother/sister, my niece and nephew.

4. Yes, sir/ma'am.

5. Yes, my brother/sister.

6. Martín/Martina Hernández.

7. The other (male/female) driver ran the red light.

8. Okay.

Follow-up

If time permits, each group should choose one of the two situations on which to focus their attention. Review the dialogue line by line and try to formulate strategies for incorporating non-offensive body language that may help the public safety official convey the meaning of the spoken Spanish phrases and expressions. Remember, facial expressions are highly effective body language, too. Your instructor may want to incorporate his/her knowledge of hand gestures that Hispanics my find offensive. Otherwise, try searching for this information on the internet and share your findings with the class.

B) Creating More Phrases and Expressions

Instructions: In the second situation from exercise A, you saw the line of dialogue said by the Spanish-speaker *"The other driver ran the red light."* To construct this phrase, you needed to find two key phrases from this section and tie them together to come up with the Spanish phrase *"El otro chofer se saltó el semáforo en rojo"*. Once you understand how to manipulate phrases and expressions already provided, creating your own will become relatively easier. By employing strategies, such as looking for cognates and words with which you are already familiar, try forming the following sentences in Spanish. After you have finished, review them as a class and allow your instructor the opportunity to provide simple explanations as to their formation to clear up any difficulties you may have encountered. Keep practicing, this is fairly advanced but nice to know and very helpful!

Example:

"The other driver ran the red light." (you know it to be "a male driver")

useful information found in numbers 33 and 35 from this section:

33. ¿Se saltó alguien el semáforo en rojo?

*35. **El otro/La otra** chofer/motorista.*

formation: El otro chofer se saltó el semáforo en rojo.

1. "The other motorist lost control of the vehicle." (you know it to be "a female motorist")

useful information found in numbers ___ and ___ from this section:

___. _____

___. _____

formation: _____

2. "An animal was to blame."

useful information found in numbers ___ and ___ from this section:

___. _____

___. _____

formation: _____

3. "There was a blowout because of the road conditions."

___. _____

___. _____

formation: _____

Cyber-Investigation

"Not crossing language and cultural barriers" was cited in **Before You Begin** as a primary problem for making Hispanics safer motorists. Browse the Internet and see what information you can find related to what efforts are being made, if any, to better this problem. What special considerations should be made when targeting the Hispanic community regarding traffic safety? What is being done on the state/federal levels? Share your findings with the class and discuss them.

Chapter 9

Miranda Rights

Before You Begin

Oftentimes, Hispanics being read their Miranda Rights do not understand them because these legal concepts are foreign to them based upon their country of origin. Issues such as non-English speaking Hispanics paired with non-Spanish speaking officers compounded with insufficient knowledge of the US legal system complicates the implementation of the Miranda Rights and may lead to someone ignorantly waiving them. Also, since Hispanics as a whole tend to be very agreeable and reluctant to admit they truly do not understand, the official reading the Miranda Rights may erroneously assume that what the person is hearing is being understood, whether it be read in English or Spanish. Checking for the individual's comprehension is imperative.

Phrases

English	Pronunciation & Spanish
1. I am going to read you your rights.	*lay boh^ee ah lay-**ayr** soos day-**ray**-chohs.* Le voy a leer sus derechos.

Miranda Rights start here:

English	Pronunciation & Spanish
2. You have the right to remain silent.	***tee^ay**-nay ayl day-**ray**-choh day goo^ahr-**dahr** see-**layn**-see^oh.* Tiene el derecho de guardar silencio.
Anything you say may be used	*koo^ahl-**kee^ayr koh**-sah kay **dee**-gah say **poo^ay**-day oo-**sahr*** Cualquier cosa que diga se puede usar
against you in a court of law.	*ayn soo **kohn**-trah ayn oon tree-boo-**nahl**.* en su contra en un tribunal.
3. You have the right to speak to an	***tee^ay**-nay ayl day-**ray**-choh day ah-**blahr** kohn* Tiene el derecho de hablar con
an attorney and to have an attorney	*oon ah-boh-**gah**-doh ee tay-**nayr** oon ah-boh-**gah**-doh* un abogado y tener un abogado
present during questioning.	*pray-**sayn**-tay doo-**rahn**-tay soo een-tay-rroh-gah-**toh**-ree^oh.* presente durante su interrogatorio.
4. If you cannot afford an attorney, one will	*see oo-**stayd** noh **poo^ay**-day koh-stay-**ahr** ah oon ah-boh-**gah**-doh,* Si Ud no puede costear a un abogado,
be provided for you at government	*ayl goh-**bee^ayr**-noh ah-seeg-nah-**rah** ee pah-gah-**rah** ah **oo**-noh **pah**-rah* el gobierno asignará y pagará a uno para

127

expense, before any questions,	*rray-pray-sayn-**tahr**-lay **ahn**-tays day soo een-tay-rroh-gah-**toh**-ree^oh,* representarle antes de su interrogatorio,
if you wish.	*see oo-**stayd** loh day-**say**-ah.* si Ud. lo desea.
5. You can decide at any time	*oo-**stayd** poo^ay-day day-see-**deer** ayn koo^ahl-**kee^ayr** moh-**mayn**-toh* Ud. puede decidir en cualquier momento
to exercise these rights and not	*ay-hayr-**sayr ay**-stohs day-**ray**-chohs ee noh* ejercer estos derechos y no
answer any questions	*kohn-tays-**tahr** neen-**goo**-nah pray-**goon**-tah* contestar ninguna pregunta
or make any statements.	*nee ah-**sayr** neen-**goo**-nah day-klah-rah-**see^ohn**.* ni hacer ninguna declaración.

Follow-up Questions and Statements:

1. Do you understand your rights?	*kohm-**prayn**-day soos day-**ray**-chohs?* ¿Comprende sus derechos?
2. It is important that you understand	*ays eem-pohr-**tahn**-tay kay kohm-**prayn**-dah* Es importante que comprenda
these rights completely	*soos day-**ray**-chohs ah **fohn**-doh* sus derechos a fondo
before you say "yes".	***ahn**-tays day day-**seer** kay see.* antes de decirnos que "sí".
3. Do you wish to remain silent (until	*pray-**fee^ay**-ray goo^ahr-**dahr** see-**layn**-see^oh* ¿Prefiere guardar silencio (hasta que
someone can explain them to you	*(**ah**-stah kay **ahl**-ghee^ayn say lohs **poo^ay**-dah ayk-splee-**kahr*** alguien se los pueda explicar
in Spanish)?	*ayn ay-spahn-**yohl**)?* en español)?
4. Do you wish to speak now?	*pray-**fee^ay**-ray ah-**blahr** ah-**oh**-rah?* ¿Prefiere hablar ahora?
5. Do you wish to wait for an attorney	*pray-**fee^ay**-ray ay-spay-**rahr** ah kay oon ah-boh-**gah**-doh* ¿Prefiere esperar a que un abogado
to be present?	*ay-**stay** pray-**sayn**-tay?* esté presente?
6. Do you wish to wait for an interpreter	*pray-**fee^ay**-ray ay-spay-**rahr** ah kay oon een-**tayr**-pray-tay* ¿Prefiere esperar a que un intérprete
to be present?	*ay-**stay** pray-**sayn**-tay?* esté presente?
7. Please cooperate fully.	*fah-**bohr** day koh-oh-pay-**rahr** kohm-play-tah-**mayn**-tay.* Favor de cooperar completamente.

Practical Activities

A) Oral Practice

Instructions: With a partner, practice reading the Miranda Rights aloud, first together, then individually. Make sure to pay close attention to the pronunciation. You may want to eventually commit them to memory if it is something you will use frequently. However, for the sake of time and practice, don't worry about memorizing now. Concentrate on proper delivery that is intelligible.

B) Matching

Instructions: Match the beginning of each phrase from the first column with the correct ending from the second column. Once you have matched the fragments, place the proper punctuation at the end to indicate whether it is a questions (?) or a statement (.). Then practice saying each phrase aloud and giving the English meaning.

1. __ ¿Prefiere esperar a ...   a. sus derechos __

2. __ ¿Prefiere hablar ...   b. un intérprete esté presente __

3. __ ¿Comprende ...   c. derechos a fondo __

4. __ ¿Prefiere guardar ...   d. coopere completamente __

5. __ ¿Prefiere esperar a que ...   e. ahora __

6. __ Es importante que comprenda ... f. silencio __

7. __ Por favor, ...   g. que un abogado esté presente __

Cyber-Investigation

Making sure that an individual is truly informed of his/her rights is a vital element of the law. You read in **Before You Begin** how a person's lack of knowledge not only of their rights but the English language can cause great confusion and problems. With this said, use the Internet to search for information that addresses this problem in more detail and perhaps provides details of a specific case in which this occurred. What happened in this case? What are your views on ensuring a person understands his/her rights? Should language be an excuse for not justly treating an individual? Share your findings and opinions with the class.

Chapter 10

Acts of Aggression and Assaults

Before You Begin

The crime rate in Latin America is double that of the world's average. With this said, one can understand how Latin America is considered one of the most violent regions in the world. Many countries report experiencing a sense of "lawlessness" due to a weakening of legal institutions. Most notably, politicians contribute greatly to the decay of judicial systems by dismissing law makers and replacing them with those who will carry out their own political agenda. Overall, there is a general lack of respect for human rights by those in charge of maintaining public order. Likewise, corruption among public safety officials perpetuate an environment of fear and distrust for the general population. This corruption has its roots in the economic uncertainty, social crises and poor education which plague many Latin American countries. Crimes such as illegal drug trafficking, money laundering/counterfeiting, and organized crime networks account for the problems associated with ineffective legal systems.

In some regions, torture has resurfaced as a means of obtaining confessions from criminal suspects, though this claim will quickly be denied by law enforcement. There is also a discriminatory attitude toward women which may be directly related to the traditional role of the female in Hispanic culture, which is confining and extremely limiting when contrasted with that of Hispanic males.

Phrases

English	Pronunciation & Spanish
1. I am —.	soh^ee—. Soy —. [1]
2. Who called for help?	kee^ayn pee-dee-**oh** ah^ee-**yoo**-dah? ¿Quién pidió ayuda?
3. (Do you know) who attacked you?	(**sah**-bay ah) kee^ayn lay ah-tah-**koh**? ¿(Sabe a) quién le atacó?
4. (Do you know) who did this to you?	(**sah**-bay ah) kee^ayn lay **ee**-soh **ay**-stoh? ¿(Sabe a) quién le hizo esto?
5. Do you know this person?	koh-**noh**-say ah **ay**-stah payr-**soh**-nah? ¿Conoce a esta persona?
6. What is your relationship with this person?	koo^ahl ays soo rray-lah-**see^ohn** kohn **ay**-stah payr-**soh**-nah? ¿Cuál es su relación con esta persona? [2]
7. Do you know where this person lives?	**sah**-bay **dohn**-day **bee**-bay **ay**-stah payr-**soh**-nah? ¿Sabe dónde vive esta persona?

8. Can you show me where?

*may **poo^ay**-day moh-**strahr dohn**-day?*
¿Me puede mostrar dónde?

9. Do you know where this person is

*sah-bay **dohn**-day ay-**stah** ay-stah payr-**soh**-nah*
¿Sabe dónde está esta persona

right now?

*ah-**oh**-rah **mees**-moh?*
ahora mismo?

10. Will you come with me and

*poo^**ay**-day bay-**neer** kohn-**mee**-goh ee*
¿Puede venir conmigo y

show me where?

*moh-**strahr**-may **dohn**-day?*
mostrarme dónde?

11. Were there any witnesses?

*ah-**bee**-ah tay-**stee**-gohs?*
¿Había testigos? [3]

12. Can you identify ...

*poo^**ay**-day een-dayn-tee-fee-**kahr** ...*
¿Puede identificar ...

the aggresor [or assailant]?

*ayl ah-gray-**sohr** / lah ah-gray-**sohr**-ah?*
el agresor / la agresora? [4]

the suspect?

*ayl soh-spay-**choh**-soh / lah soh-spay-**choh**-sah?*
el sospechoso / la sospechosa? [5]

the perpetrator?

*ayl payr-pay-trah-**dohr** / lah payr-pay-trah-**doh**-rah?*
el perpetrador / la perpetradora? [6]

the attacker?

*ayl/lah ah-tah-**kahn**-tay?*
el/la atacante?

13. Were you ...

foo^ay ...
¿Fue

physically assaulted?

*ah-tah-**kah**-doh/dah **fee**-see-kah-mayn-tay?*
atacado/a físicamente? [7]

hit?

*pay-**gah**-doh/dah?*
pegado/da? [7]

stabbed?

*ah-poon-yah-**lah**-doh/dah?*
apuñalado/a? [7]

attacked with an object?

*ah-tah-**kah**-doh/dah kohn ahl-**goon** ohb-**hay**-toh?*
atacado/a con algún objeto? [7]

attacked with a weapon?

*ah-tah-**koh** kohn ahl-**goo**-nah **ahr**-mah?*
atacado/a con alguna arma? [7,8]

shot?

*pay-**gah**-doh/dah oon dee-**spah**-roh?*
pegado/a un disparo? [7]

Was it a drive-by?

*foo^ay oon dee-**spah**-roh day oon bay-ee-koo-loh?*
Fue un disparo de un vehículo?

robbed?

*rroh-**bah**-doh/dah?*
robado/a? [7]

(sexually) harrassed?	*ah-koh-**sah**-doh/dah (sayk-soo^ahl-**mayn**-tay)?* acosado/a (sexualmente)? [7,9]
injured?	*ay-**ree**-doh/dah?* herido/a? [7]
(verbally/physically) threatened?	*ah-may-nah-**sah**-doh/dah (bayr-bahl-**mayn**-tay / **fee**-see-kah-mayn-tay)?* amenazado/a (verbalmente/físicamente)? [7]
burned with something?	*kay-**mah**-doh/dah kohn **ahl**-goh?* quemado/a con algo? [7]
tortured?	*tohr-too-**rah**-doh/dah?* torturado/a? [7]

14. Show me where.	***moo^ay**-stray-may **dohn**-day.* Muéstreme dónde.
15. Can you describe this person physically?	***poo^ay**-day day-skree-**beer** ah **ay**-stah payr-**soh**-nah **fee**-see-kah-mayn-tay?* ¿Puede describir a esta persona físicamente? [10]
16. Have you had problems with this person before?	*ah tay-**nee**-doh proh-**blay**-mahs kohn **ay**-stah* ¿Ha tenido problemas con esta *payr-**soh**-nah **ahn**-tays?* persona antes?
17. Have you ever seen this person before?	*ah bee-stoh **ahn**-tays ah **ay**-stah payr-**soh**-nah?* ¿Ha visto antes a esta persona?
18. In the neighborhood?	*ayn ayl bay-seen-**dah**-ree^oh / **bah**-rree^oh?* ¿En el vecindario / barrio?
19. At ...	*ayn ...* ¿En ...
a department store?	*oon ahl-mah-**sayn**?* un almacén?
a mall/shopping center?	*oon **sayn**-troh koh-mayr-**see^ahl**?* un centro comercial?
a grocery store?	*oon soo-payr-mayr-**kah**-doh?* un supermercado?
an event?	*oon ay-**bayn**-toh?* un evento?
a park?	*oon **pahr**-kay?* un parque?
a school?	*oo-nah ay-**skoo^ay**-lah?* una escuela?
public?	*poo-blee-koh?* público?

20. Do you remember the name of

   *rray-**koo**^**ayr**-dah ayl **nohm**-bray dayl loo-**gahr***
   ¿Recuerda el nombre del lugar

   the place where you saw

   ***dohn**-day bee^oh ah*
   dónde vio a

   this person?

   ***ay**-stah payr-**soh**-nah?*
   esta persona?

---

21. I need to file a police report.

   *nay-say-**see**-toh ay-mee-**teer** oon een-**fohr**-may poh-lee-**see**^ahl.*
   Necesito emitir un informe policial.

---

22. This is your police report number.

   ***ay**-stay ays ayl **noo**-may-roh day soo een-**fohr**-may poh-lee-**see**^ahl.*
   Este es el número de su informe policial.

---

23. You can obtain a copy at the

   ***poo**^**ay**-day ohb-tay-**nayr** oo-nah **koh**-pee^ah day lah*
   Puede obtener una copia de la

   police department.

   *koh-mee-sah-**ree**-ah.*
   comisaría.

---

24. Do you want to press charges?

   ***kee**^**ay**-ray pray-sayn-**tahr kahr**-gohs?*
   ¿Quiere presentar cargos?

---

25. Do you want me to arrest the person?

   ***kee**^**ay**-ray kay ah-**rray**-stay ah **ay**-stah payr-**soh**-nah?*
   ¿Quiere que arreste a esta persona?

---

26. Do you want to drop the charges?

   ***kee**^**ay**-ray rray-tee-**rahr** lohs **kahr**-gohs?*
   ¿Quiere retirar los cargos?

---

27. I have a warrant for the arrest of—.

   ***tayn**-goh oo-nah **ohr**-dayn day ah-**rray**-stoh **pah**-rah—.*
   Tengo una orden de arresto para—.

---

28. I have a search warrant.

   ***tayn**-goh oo-nah **ohr**-dayn day rray-**hee**-stroh.*
   Tengo una orden de registro.

---

29. Please cooperate fully.

   *pohr fah-**bohr** koh-oh-**pay**-ray kohm-play-tah-**mayn**-tay.*
   Por favor, coopere completamente.

---

30. I am not going to do you any harm.

   *noh lay boh^ee ah ah-**sayr** neen-**goon dahn**-yoh.*
   No le voy a hacer ningún daño.

---

31. You will have to come with me.

   *tayn-**drah** kay bay-**neer** kohn-**mee**-goh.*
   Tendrá que venir conmigo. [11]

---

32. You are being taken to this location.

   *lay ay-**stoh**^**ee** yay-**bahn**-doh ah **ay**-stah loh-kah-lee-sah-**see**^ohn.*
   Le estoy llevando a esta localización.

---

33. I didn't do anything wrong.

   *noh **ee**-say **nah**-dah **mah**-loh.*
   No hice nada malo.

Notes

[1] Use the appropriate job title from *Chapter 1 - Identifying Yourself and Preliminary Scene Assessment.*

[2] See *Chapter 15 - Family and Friends* for useful vocabulary.

[3] See *Chapter 8 - Routine Traffic Situations - Traffic Accidents and Calling for Emergency Assistance* for expressions used to speak to witnesses.

[4] Use *el agresor* for a *male* and *la agresora* for a *female*.

[5] Use *el sospechoso* for a *male* and *la sospechosa* for a *female*.

[6] Use *el perpetrador* for a *male* and *la la perpetradora* for a *female*.

[7] Use the *-o ending* for *males* and the *-a ending* for *females*.

[8] See *Chapter 7 - Threats, Dangers and Alerts - Weapons* for a list of commonly used weapons.

[9] The term *hostigado/a (oh-stee-**gah**-doh/dah)* is a synonym for *acosado/a*.

[10] Familiarity with *Chapter 3 - Physical and Personal Descriptions* and *Chapter 3 - Physical and Personal Descriptions - Clothing, Accessories and Colors* is especially helpful here. You may use these referenced chapters to ask "yes" and "no" questions in Spanish about the person.

[11] Reference *Chapter 9 - Miranda Rights* for continuation of this process.

Practical Activities

Acts of Aggression and Assaults

A) Oral Practice

Instructions: In groups of three or four, have two people stand and act out the situation as a third person or other pair reads aloud the prompts one-by-one according to the criteria given for each situation. Remember, the pair acting out the situation may only use SPANISH. Depending upon how familiar the actors are with the material, they may choose to use or not use the text for reference. Pairs/partners switch to act out the same situation again before moving on to the next one.

1. A public safety official introduces him/herself, asks who called for help, asks if the victim knows the attacker, what is the victim's relationship to the attacker and where that person lives.

2. The public safety official asks if the victim can identify the attacker, then asks the victim how he/she was attacked. Finally the victim is asked if he/she can describe the attacker physically.

3. Continuing, the official asks if the victim has ever had problems with the attacker before, where this person may have been seen; then, informs the victim a police report will be filed. In conclusion, the official gives the victim the police report number and explains where a copy of the report may be obtained.

B) Talking with the Suspect

Instructions: Translate the dialogue that takes place between the officer and the suspect upon arriving at the suspect's residence. Then review your translation with a partner and make any necessary corrections.

agente: Buenos días, Soy el agente Ramsey. ¿Está el Sr. Torres? _____

_____

Sr. Torres: Soy yo. ¿Por qué? _____

agente: Tengo una orden de arresto para el Sr. Torres. _____

_____

Sr. Torres: ¿Por qué? No hice nada malo. _____

agente: Lo siento, señor. No hablo mucho español. Por favor, coopere completamente. No le voy a hacer ningún

daño. _____

_____

Sr. Torres: No entiendo. No es justo. _____

agente: Tendrá que venir conmigo. Le estoy llevando a esta localización. _____

_____

Rape, Sexual Assault and Domestic Violence

Before You Begin:

Gender roles in Hispanic and Latino culture are often strictly defined. From very early on in life, male and female children are socialized differently. Whereas females are raised to be nurturing and sensitive, males are taught to be dominant and authoritative. The expectation of a strong, domineering male is a traditional cultural norm which is widely accepted. This culturally imposed male role is commonly denominated "machismo" (a patriarchal dominance of the household and family) and is directly attributed to females having to deal with discrimination in every aspect of their lives. It has even been stated that "machismo" leads to women being objectified sexually as well as encouraging physical abuse against them. While the idea of a male providing for his wife and family may be not be conceptually negative, it does promote an environment in which a male may easily shift in behavior from assertive to physically aggressive.

Should you have to deal with a Hispanic female who has been sexually violated or physically attacked, make sure to be culturally sensitive. Make every effort to have another female available with whom she can speak or ask her if she would prefer to speak with a female then send for one and advise her one is one the way. Hispanic females are even somewhat shy about visiting doctors for standard health examinations and given the gravity of a physical attack, be it sexual in nature or not, she will feel much more comfortable speaking with someone of the same sex.

Phrases

English	Pronunciation & Spanish
1. I am —.	*soh^ee—.* Soy —. [1]
2. Do you prefer to speak with a female?	*pray-**fee^ay**-ray ah-**blahr** kohn **oo**-nah moo-**hayr**?* ¿Prefiere hablar con una mujer?
3. I'm sending for a female officer.	*pay-dee-**ray** kay **mahn**-dayn ah oo-nah ah-**hayn**-tay day poh-lee-**see**-ah.* Pediré que manden a una agente de policía.
4. I know this is difficult, but we have to	*say kay **ay**-stoh ays dee-**fee**-seel **pay**-roh tay-**nay**-mohs* Sé que esto es difícil, pero tenemos
ask you	*kay ah-**sayr**-lay* que hacerle
some questions.	*ahl-**goo**-nahs pray-**goon**-tahs.* algunas preguntas.
5. Take your time.	***toh**-may soo **tee^aym**-poh.* Tome su tiempo.
6. Were you attacked by more than	*foo^ay ah-tah-**kah**-doh/dah pohr mahs day* ¿Fue atacado/a por más de
one person?	***oo**-nah payr-**soh**-nah?* una persona? [2]

7. Were you ...

foo^ay ...
¿Fue ...

    sexually assaulted?

*ah-gray-**dee**-doh/dah sayk-soo^ahl-**mayn**-tay?*
agredido/a sexualmente? [2]

    raped?

*bee^oh-**lah**-doh/dah?*
violado/a? [2]

---

8. How many were there?

***koo^ayn**-tahs payr-**soh**-nahs ah-**bee**-ah?*
¿Cuántas personas había?

---

9. Male(s)?

***ohm**-bray(s)?*
¿Hombre(s)?

---

10. Female(s)?

*moo-**hayr**-(ays)?*
¿Mujer(es)?

---

11. Did they force you/Were you forced ...

*lay fohr-**sah**-rohn ah ...*
¿Le forzaron a ...

    to get undressed?

*days-noo-**dahr**-say?*
desnudarse?

    to perform obscene acts?

*ray-ah-lee-**sahr ahk**-tohs ohb-**say**-nohs?*
realizar actos obscenos?

    to have intercourse/sexual relations?

*tay-**nayr koh^ee**-toh / rray-lah-**see^oh**-nays sayk-**soo^ah**-lays?*
tener coito / relaciones sexuales?

    to have oral sex?

*tay-**nayr sayk**-soh oh-**rahl?***
tener sexo oral?

    to have anal sex?

*tay-**nayr sayk**-soh ah-**nahl?***
tener sexo anal?

    to masturbate him/her?

*mahs-toor-**bahr**-lay?*
masturbarle?

    to masturbate in front of him / her?

*mahs-toor-**bahr**-lay ahn-tay ayl / **ay**-yah?*
masturbarse ante él / ella?

---

12. Did they make you/Were you forced

*lay fohr-**sah**-rohn*
¿Le forzaron

    to watch them have sex ...

*ah mee-**rahr mee^ayn**-trahs tay-**nee**-ahn **sayk**-soh ...*
a mirar mientras tenían sexo ...

        with another person?

*kohn **oh**-trah payr-**soh**-nah?*
con otra persona?

        with an animal?

*kohn oon ah-nee-**mahl?***
con un animal?

        with a sex toy?

*kohn ahl-**goon** hoo-**gay**-tay sayk-**soo^ahl?***
con algún juguete sexual?

13. Were you …	*foo^ay …* ¿Fue …
restrained?	*rray-streen-**hee**-doh/dah?* restringido/a? [2]
physically abused?	*ah-boo-**sah**-doh/dah **fee**-see-kah-mayn-tay?* abusado/a físicamente? [2]
drugged?	*droh-**gah**-doh/dah?* drogado/a? [2]
strangled?	*ay-strahn-goo-**lah**-doh/dah?* estrangulado/a? [2]
kidnapped?	*say-koo^ay-**strah**-doh/dah?* secuestrado/a? [2]
bitten?	*morh-**dee**-doh/dah?* mordido/a? [2]
threatened?	*ah-may-nah-**sah**-doh/dah?* amenazado/a? [2]
14. Were you unconscious?	*ay-**stoo**-boh days-mah-**yah**-doh/dah?* ¿Estuvo desmayado/a? [2]
15. Were you penetrated (with an object)?	*foo^ay pay-nay-**trah**-doh/dah (kohn ahl-**goon** ohb-**hay**-toh)?* ¿Fue penetrado/a (con algún objeto)? [2]
16. Were you fondled?	*foo^ay ah-kah-ree-**see^ah**-doh/dah seen kay-**rayr**?* ¿Fue acariciado/a sin querer? [2]
17. Did they fondle your / Were your …	*lay ah-kah-ree-**see^ah**-rohn …* Le acariciaron …
breasts?	*lohs **say**-nohs?* los senos?
genitals?	*lohs hay-nee-**tah**-lays?* los genitales?
18. Were you / he / she soliciting sex?	*soh-lee-see-**tah**-bah oo-**stayd** / ayl / **ay** yah **sayk**-soh?* ¿Solicitaba Ud. / él / ella sexo?
19. Were you / he / she prostituting?	*proh-stee-too-**ee**-ah oo-**stayd** / ayl / **ay**-yah?* ¿Prostituía Ud. / él / ella?
20. Were you/was he/was she paid	*lay pah-**gah**-rohn* ¿Le pagaron
to have sex?	*pohr **sayk**-soh?* por sexo?
21. Were you offered … for sex?	*lay oh-fray-**see^ay**-rohn … pohr **sayk**-soh?* ¿Le ofrecieron … por sexo?
money	*dee-**nay**-roh* dinero

drugs	*droh-gahs* drogas
alcohol	*ahl-koh-**ohl*** alcohol
gifts	*rray-**gah**-lohs* regalos
favors	*fah-**boh**-rays* favores
protection/security	*say-goo-ree-**dahd*** seguridad

---

22. Did you accept anything from them?
*ah-sayp-**toh** koo^ahl-**kee^ayr** koh-sah day ay-yohs?*
¿Aceptó cualquier cosa de ellos?

---

23. Do you have a pimp?
***tee^ay**-nay prohk-say-**nay**-tah / ahl-kah-**oo^ay**-tay?*
¿Tiene proxeneta / alcahuete?

---

24. Did your pimp do this to you?
*lay **ee**-soh **ay**-stoh soo prohk-say-**nay**-tah / ahl-kah-**oo^ay**-tay?*
¿Le hizo esto su proxeneta / alcahuete?

---

25. Are you sure this information is
*ay-**stah** say-**goo**-roh/rah kay **ay**-stah een-fohr-mah-**see^ohn** say-ah*
¿Está seguro/a que esta información sea

correct?
*koh-**rrayk**-tah?*
correcta? [2]

---

26. Do you have any doubts?
***tee^ay**-nay koo^ahl-**kee^ayr** doo-dah?*
¿Tiene cualquier duda?

---

27. Have you cleaned yourself up
*say ah leem-**pee^ah**-doh **days**-day*
¿Se ha limpiado desde

since this happened?
*kay **ay**-stoh lay pah-**soh**?*
que esto le pasó?

---

28. It's important that you
*ays eem-pohr-**tahn**-tay kay*
Es importante que

do not clean yourself up yet.
*noh say **leem**-pee^ay pohr ayl moh-**mayn**-toh.*
no se limpie por el momento.

---

29. A medical professional
*oon/**oo**-nah proh-fay-see^oh-**nahl** **may**-dee-koh/**may**-dee-kah*
Un / una profesional médico/médica

will need to examine you first.
*lay nay-say-see-tah-**rah** ah-**sayr** oon ayk-**sah**-mayn **may**-dee-koh pree-**may**-roh.*
le necesitará hacer un examen médico primero.

---

30. The examination ...
*ayl ayk-**sah**-mayn **may**-dee-koh ...*
El examen médico ...

is for your own protection.
*ays **pah**-rah soo **proh**-pee^ah proh-tayk-**see^ohn**.*
es para su propia protección.

will help us collect evidence.
*nohs ah^ee-yoo-dah-**rah** ah rray-koh-**hayr** proo^ay-bah.*
nos ayudará a recoger prueba.

31. Please, stay here.	*pohr fah-**bohr** **kay**-day-say ah-**kee**.* Por favor, quédese aquí.
32. I have someone coming to help you.	*ay pay-**dee**-doh kay **ahl**-ghee^ayn **bayn**-gah ah ah^ee-oo-**dahr**-lay.* He pedido que alguien venga a ayudarle.
33. Is there anyone you would like to call?	*ah^ee **ahl**-ghee^ayn kay kee-**see^ay**-rah yah-**mahr**?* ¿Hay alguien que quisiera llamar?
34. Would you like for us to take you to a (woman's) shelter?	*kee-**see^ay**-rah kay lay yay-**bah**-rah-mohs ah* ¿Quisera que le lleváramos a *oon ahl-**bayr**-gay (**pah**-rah moo-**hay**-rays)?* un albergue (para mujeres)?
35. Do you have somewhere to go?	***tee^ay**-nay ah-**dohn**-day eer?* ¿Tiene adónde ir?
36. Will you be alright if I leave?	*bah ah ay-**stahr** bee^ayn see may boh^ee?* ¿Va a estar bien si me voy?
37. Call again if you need us to come back.	***yah**-may **oh**-trah bays see nay-say-**see**-tah kay bohl-**bah**-mohs.* Llame otra vez si necesita que volvamos.

Notes

[1] Identify yourself with the proper title from *Chapter 1 - Identifying Yourself* and *Preliminary Scene Assessment* where appropriate. Also, feel free to reference past chapters especially *Chapter 2 - Multipurpose Interview for Personal Data and Information, Chapter 3 - Physical and Personal Descriptions, Chapter 4 - Useful Commands and Chapter 10 - Acts of Aggression and Assault* to assist you in obtaining pertinent information and taking control of the situation.

[2] Use the *-o ending* for *males* and the *-a ending* for *females*.

Practical Activities

Rape, Sexual Assault and Domestic Violence

A) Oral Practice

Instructions: Regardless of your job title and responsibilities, it is highly possible most public safety officials will come into contact with the victim of a violent crime at some point in time. Taking into account the information you read in **Before You Begin,** prepare what the officer would ask/say to the victim in each possible scenario using 2-3 phrases/expressions from this section. Also, consider how the officer's tone of voice and body language will influence the way in which these phrases and expressions are received as well as the gender of both the officer and the victim.

1. A male officer encounters a female victim when responding to a call. He is concerned she may not feel comfortable speaking with him.
2. A female officer is asking a possible female rape victim about the nature of the attack.
3. A male inmate is assaulted by other inmates while showering. The officer must find out what occurred.
4. A female officer suspects that a female inmate was forcibly restrained by two or more other inmates and asks questions for more detail.
5. A male victim is found slightly conscious in an alleyway by an officer. The victim appears to have been physically beaten and possibly violated.
6. A female calls the police alleging a stranger followed her home, restrained her and robbed her.
7. A badly beaten suspected prostitute is found by a female officer. The officer first suspects the female's pimp.
8. You must give advice to the victim of a rape not to destroy what could be physical evidence. You also explain to the victim why a medical exam is necessary.

B) Multipurpose Phrases and Expressions

Instructions: You may have noticed throughout this text that many times the beginning of a phrase/expression *(phrase starters)* has multiple uses and can be paired with other information to create a completely different question or statement. An example with which you are already familiar is "*¿Cuál es su ...*" which can be paired with a number of other *phrase completers* such as: "*nombre; estado civil; dirección; número de teléfono; etc.*". Remembering phrases based on function instead of individually as a separate unit will make retention much easier. Below, are some *phrase starters* from this section. Say aloud all of the possible *phrase completers* from this section for each of the respective *phrase starters*. Write them out as well, if you choose. Then practice their English meaning by saying them aloud.

1. ¿Fue ...

2. ¿Le forzaron a ...

3. ¿Le acariciaron ...

4. ¿Le ofrecieron ...

5. El examen médico ...

Chapter 11

Criminal Activity

Dealing with Juveniles/Minors[1]

Before You Begin

The school dropout rate is higher among Latinos (Latino, in this case, meaning anyone from a Latin American country, including those whose primary language is not Spanish, such as Brazil) than any other racial or ethnic group. In comparison, Latinos rank second highest in the use of alcohol, binge drinking and heavy alcohol use. Among the many risk factors that contribute to these findings are poverty, family management problems, communication barriers as well as discrimination and acculturation difficulties. Current research also shows an increase in substance use by Latino youth, although as a whole among U.S. adolescents, substance use has dropped. Alcohol remains the primary substance used by Latino adolescents, while tobacco use ranks as a very close second. Regarding adolescent Latina females who were pregnant, six out of ten Latinas reported using beer or wine before the end of their first trimester of pregnancy, while half reported using marijuana.

Phrases

English	Pronunciation & Spanish
1. (There is reason to believe) …	*(ah^ee rah-**sohn pah**-rah kray-**ayr** kay)* … (Hay razón para creer que) …
you have broken the law.	*ahs kay-brahn-**tah**-doh lah lay^ee.* has quebrantado la ley.
your — has broken the law.	*soo — ah kay-brahn-**tah**-doh lah lay^ee.* su — ha quebrantado la ley. [2]
2. You have / (S)he has committed …	*ahs / ah koh-may-**tee**-doh …* Has / Ha cometido …
a felony …	*oon day-**lee**-toh mah-**yohr** / **grah**-bay …* un delito mayor / grave …
a misdemeanor …	*oon day-**lee**-toh may-**nohr** …* un delito menor …
a crime …	*oon day-**lee**-toh …* un delito … [3]
a capital crime …	*oon **kree**-mayn …* un crimen … [3]

147

3. … according to …

*… say-**goon** …*
… según …

    state law.

*lah lay^ee ay-stah-**tahl**.*
la ley estatal.

    federal law.

*lah lay^ee fay-day-**rahl**.*
la ley federal.

4. Do you speak (any) English?

*ah-blahs (oon **poh**-koh day) een-**glays**?*
¿Hablas (un poco de) inglés?

5. I am going …

tay boh^ee ah …
Te voy a …

    to read you your Miranda rights.

*lay-**ayr** toos day-**ray**-chohs Miranda.*
leer tus derechos Miranda.

    to call for an interpreter.

*pay-**deer** ah oon een-**tayr**-pray-tay.*
pedir a un intérprete.

6. Due to your age, you are considered a juvenile/minor.

*day-**bee**-doh ah too ay-**dahd** tay kohn-see-**day**-rahn may-**nohr** day ay-**dahd**.*
Debido a tu edad, te consideran menor de edad.

7. A juvenile/minor is someone under the age of …

*oon may-**nohr** day ay-**dahd** ays **ahl**-ghee^ayn **may**-nohs day …*
Un menor de edad es alguien menos de …

    16 years old.

*dee^ays ee say^ees **ahn**-yohs day ay-**dahd**.*
16 años de edad.

    17 years old.

*dee^ays ee **see^ay**-tay **ahn**-yohs day ay-**dahd**.*
17 años de edad.

    18 years old.

*dee^ays ee **oh**-choh **ahn**-yohs day ay-**dahd**.*
18 años de edad.

    21 years old.

***bay^een**-tay ee oon **ahn**-yohs day ay-**dahd**.*
21 años de edad.

8. Who …

kee^ayn …
¿Quién …

    is your legal guardian?

*ays too too-**tohr** lay-**gahl**?*
es tu tutor legal?

    bought this for you?

*tay loh kohm-**proh**?*
te lo compró?

    gave this to you?

*tay dee^oh **ay**-stoh?*
te dio esto?

9. A legal guardian must be present

*oon too-**tohr** lay-**gahl** day-bay day ay-**stahr** pray-**sayn**-tay*
Un tutor legal debe de estar presente

    during (police) questioning.

*doo-**rahn**-tay oon een-tay-rroh-gah-**toh**-ree^oh (poh-lee-**see^ahl**).*
durante un interrogatorio (policial).

10. Can I contact your (legal) guardian

*poo^ay-doh koh-moo-nee-**kahr**-may kohn too too-**tohr** (lay-**gahl**)*
¿Puedo comunicarme con tu tutor (legal)

    by phone?

*pohr tay-**lay**-foh-noh?*
por teléfono?

---

11. What's the phone number?

*koo^ahl ays ayl **noo**-may-roh day tay-**lay**-foh-noh?*
¿Cuál es el número de teléfono?

---

12. Where do you live?

*dohn-day **bee**-bays?*
¿Dónde vives?

---

13. Write the address here.

*ay-**skree**-bay lah dee-rayk-**see^ohn** ah-**kee**.*
Escribe la dirección aquí.

---

14. You can make a phone call ...

*poo^**ay**-days ah-**sayr** oo-nah yah-**mah**-dah tay-lay-**foh**-nee-kah …*
Puedes hacer una llamada telefónica …

    from the county jail.

*day lah **kahr**-sayl dayl kohn-**dah**-doh.*
de la cárcel del condado.

    from the police station.

*day lah koh-mee-sah-**ree**-ah.*
de la comisaría.

---

15. Due to his/her age, he/she is considered a juvenile/minor.

*day-**bee**-doh ah soo ay-**dahd** say lay kohn-see-**day**-rah may-**nohr** day ay-**dahd**.*
Debido a su edad, se le considera menor de edad.

---

16. The legal treatment of a juvenile

*ayl trah-tah-**mee^ayn**-toh lay-**gahl** day oon may-**nohr** day ay-**dahd***
El tratamiento legal de un menor de edad

    is different than that of an adult.

*ays dee-fay-**rayn**-tay kay ayl day oon mah-**yohr** day ay-**dahd**.*
es diferente que el de un mayor de edad.

---

17. I am going to warn and release you (this time).

*tay boh^ee ah dahr oon ah-**bee**-soh ee sohl-**tahr**-tay (**ay**-stah bays).*
Te voy a dar un aviso y soltarte (esta vez).

---

18. I am going to detain you until your

*tay boh^ee ah day-tay-**nayr** ah-stah kay **bayn**-gah too*
Te voy a detener hasta que venga tu

    (legal) guardian comes for you.

*too-**tohr** (lay-**gahl**) **pah**-rah rray-koh-**hayr**-tay.*
tutor (legal) para recogerte.

---

19. I am going to ...

tay boh^ee ah …
Te voy a …

    arrest you.

*ah-rray-**stahr**.*
arrestar.

    detain you.

*day-tay-**nayr**.*
detener.

---

20. I have an order from the court for the arrest of —.

***tayn**-goh **oo**-nah **ohr**-dayn hoo-dee-**see^ahl** **pah**-rah ayl ah-**rray**-stoh day —.*
Tengo una orden judicial para el arresto de —.

21. I have to take you into custody.

*tay **tayn**-goh kay ah-rray-**stahr.***
Te tengo que arrestar.

22. I have to arrest him/her.

*lay **tayn**-goh kay ah-rray-**stahr.***
Le tengo que arrestar.

23. I am going to take you to the county jail

*tay boh^ee ah yay-**bahr** ah lah **kahr**-sayl dayl kohn-**dah**-doh **pah**-rah*
Te voy a llevar a la cárcel del condado para

for processing.

*fee-**chahr**-tay.*
ficharte. [4]

24. He/She is going to the county jail for
processing.

*bah ah eer ah lah **kahr**-sayl dayl kohn-**dah**-doh **pah**-rah sayr fee-**chah**-doh/dah.*
Va a ir a la cárcel del condado para ser fichado/a.[4,5]

25. I am going to refer you to juvenile court.

*tay boh^ee ah mahn-**dahr** ahl tree-boo-**nahl** hoo-bay-**neel**.*
Te voy a mandar al tribunal juvenil.

26. He/She is going to go to juvenile court.

*bah ah eer ahl tree-boo-**nahl** hoo-bay-**neel**.*
Va a ir al tribunal juvenil.

27. I am going to refer you to a

*tay boh^ee ah rray-koh-mayn-**dahr** ah oon*
Te voy a recomendar a un

juvenile court probation officer.

*ah-**hayn**-tay day lee-bayr-**tahd** bee-hee-**lah**-dah dayl tree-boo-**nahl***
agente de libertad vigilada del tribunal

*pah-rah may-**noh**-rays.*
para menores.

28. I am going to refer a

*boy^ee ah rray-koh-mayn-**dahr** ah oon*
Voy a recomendar a un

juvenile court probation officer.

*ah-**hayn**-tay day lee-bayr-**tahd** bee-hee-**lah**-dah dayl tree-boo-**nahl***
agente de libertad vigilada del tribunal

*pah-rah may-**noh**-rays.*
para menores.

29. I am going to send you to a

*tay boh^ee ah mahn-**dahr** ah oon*
Te voy a mandar a un

Corrections Facility/Detention Center

*koh-rrayk-see^oh-**nahl** / **sayn**-troh day day-tayn-**see^ohn***
correccional / centro de detención

for minors/juveniles.

*pah-rah may-**noh**-rays day ay-**dahd**.*
para menores de edad.

30. He/She is going to a

bah ah eer ah oon
Va a ir a un

Corrections Facility/Detention Center

*koh-rrayk-see^oh-**nahl** / **sayn**-troh day day-tayn-**see^ohn***
correccional / centro de detención

for minors/juveniles.

*pah-rah may-**noh**-rays day ay-**dahd**.*
para menores de edad.

	*ah-**kay**-yohs may-**noh**-rays ah-koo-**sah**-dohs doo-**rahn**-tay*
31. Minors accused in	Aquellos menores acusados durante
	*oon proh-**say**-soh day day-leen-**koo^ayn**-see^ah hoo-bay-**neel***
a juvenile delinquency proceeding	un proceso de delincuencia juvenil
	*tee^**ay**-nayn …*
have …	tienen …
	*ayl day-**ray**-choh ah day-**bee**-doh proh-**say**-soh.*
the right to due process.	el derecho a debido proceso.
	*ayl day-**ray**-choh ah rray-pray-sayn-tah-**see^ohn** lay-**gahl**.*
the right to legal representation.	el derecho a representación legal.
	*ayl day-**ray**-choh **kohn**-trah lah ah^oo-toh-een-kree-mee-nah-**see^ohn**.*
the right against self-incrimination.	el derecho contra la autoincriminación.
	*noh **gree**-tays.*
32. Don't scream.	No grites.
	***kah**-yah-tay.*
33. Be quiet.	Cállate.
	***see^ayn**-tah-tay.*
34. Sit down.	Siéntate.
	***ay**-stah-tay **kee^ay**-toh/tah.*
35. Be still.	Estate quieto/a. [5]
	***kahl**-mah-tay.*
36. Calm down.	Cálmate.
	*koh-oh-**pay**-rah kohm-play-tah-**mayn**-tay.*
37. Cooperate fully.	Coopera completamente.

Notes

[1] In *Chapter 11 - Dealing with Juveniles/Minors*, phrases and expressions have been written for speaking directly to the minor as well as speaking directly to the minor's guardian. The forms are different because Spanish uses an *informal* register when an adult is addressing teens or children and a *formal* register when a professional adult is addressing another adult. The phrases and expressions in this chapter that are impersonal may be said to children, teens and adults. However, the phrases and expressions that contain *he/she* are phrases that would be said to the minor's guardian(s). All other phrases and expressions are meant to be said directly to the minor. Consult past chapters for other phrases you may need to make requests, yet do not distinguish between minors and adults. For example, *requesting I.D.* from *Chapter 8 – Routine Traffic Situations – Traffic Stops and Violations.*

[2] See *Chapter 15 – Family and Friends* for relationships.

[3] The word *crimen (**kree**-mayn)* should only be used when speaking of a capital crime such as murder. Otherwise, the general term for *crime* is *delito.*

[4] The word for *processing* in this case is *fichar.* The cognate *procesar* is false and actually means *to prosecute; to try* or *to arraign.*

[5] Use the *–o* ending when speaking to a *male* and the *–a* ending when speaking to a *female.*

Practical Activities

Dealing with Juveniles/Minors

A) Oral Practice

Instructions: You are having to deal with a minor who has broken the law while at the same time explain what is going on to the legal guardian. Using the information given below, prepare what you will say to both persons. Remember to review the information you read in the **Notes** for this section to understand why the speech used to address the minor is different than that used to address an adult. You may need to reference past chapters for additional phrases and expressions. Once you have put this information together in Spanish, form groups of three to four people and compare what you have. Make any necessary changes and/or corrections.

I. Juvenile/Minor

a. Do you speak English? (reply is no)

b. You have committed a misdemeanor according to state law.

c. Due to your age you are considered a juvenile/minor.

d. Who is your legal guardian? ...
e. What's the phone number? ...
f. Where do you live? ...
g. Write the address here.

h. I am going to refer you to juvenile court and to a juvenile court probation officer.

i. I am going to send you to a Juvenile Detention Facility until a legal guardian comes for you.

j. Cooperate fully.

II. Legal Guardian

a. Do you speak English? (reply is no)

b. Your son has committed a misdemeanor according to state law.

c. Due to his age, he is considered a juvenile/minor.

d. He is going to the county jail for processing and he is going to a Juvenile Detention Facility.

e. He is going to juvenile court and I am referring a juvenile court probation officer.

f. Minors accused in a juvenile delinquency proceeding have the right to due process and legal representation.

g. Here is the address and telephone number of the Juvenile Detention Facility.

Follow-up

Instructions: In the same group, have each member take a turn reading a random phrase from this exercise aloud in Spanish. The other members should decide if this phrase is being said to the *juvenile/minor* or the *legal guardian*. After the person to whom the phrase is directed has correctly identified it, have someone volunteer to provide the English translation aloud.

B) Matching

Instructions: Match the Spanish phrases with the English meaning below them. Then practice saying each phrase aloud and give the English translation.

1. __ Te voy a pedir a un intérprete.

2. __ Un tutor legal debe de estar presente durante un interrogatorio policial.

3. __ Tengo una orden judicial para el arresto de su hijo.

4. __ Te voy a dar un aviso y soltarte esta vez.

5. __ Aquellos menores acusados durante un proceso de delincuencia tienen el derecho contra la autoincriminación.

6. __ Aquellos menores acusados durante un proceso de delincuencia tienen el derecho a representación legal.

7. __ Te voy a llevar a la cárcel del condado para ficharte.

8. __ Va a ir a la cárcel del condado para ser fichado.

9. __ Va a ir a la cárcel del condado para ser fichada.

10. __ Le tengo que arrestar.

a. I am going to warn and release you this time.

b. Minors accused in a juvenile delinquency proceeding have the right to legal representation.

c. I am going to take you to the county jail for processing.

d. I am going to call for an interpreter.

e. He is going to the county jail for processing.

f. She is going to the county jail for processing.

g. A legal guardian must be present during police questioning.

h. I have to arrest him.

i. I have an order from the court for the arrest of your son.

j. Minors accused in a juvenile delinquency proceeding have the right against self-incrimination

Cyber-Investigation

In **Before You Begin**, you read about some of the factors that contribute to the delinquency of Hispanic/Latino youth. Further research this topic and find out more about the difficulties this group faces and how these contributing factors vary and/or are similar to those faced by other peer groups; i.e. Caucasian youth, African American youth, native American youth, etc. Share this information in small discussion groups. Allow each group member an opportunity to express his/her opinions regarding his/her findings. Lastly, discuss how this information may be beneficial for those public safety officials who work directly or indirectly with at risk youths, especially the Hispanic population.

Misdemeanors and Felonies

Before You Begin

Crime in many Latin American cities has become commonplace. The frequency with which car jackings, burglaries, muggings and homicides occur is shocking. Therefore, it is not surprising that crime-related violence is the biggest threat to public health in Latin America (more so than HIV/AIDS or any other infectious disease). In a recent study, the Center for Development Studies discovered that 96% of crimes throughout all of Latin America went unpunished between 1996 and 2003. In Mexico alone, it was found that 75% of crimes went unreported.

Phrases

English	Pronunciation & Spanish
1. (We have reason to believe) you have broken the law.	*(kray-**ay**-mohs kay) ah kay-brahn-**tah**-doh lah lay^ee.* (Creemos que) ha quebrantado la ley.
2. You have committed ...	*ah koh-may-**tee**-doh ...* Ha cometido ...
a felony ...	*oon day-**lee**-toh mah-**yohr** / **grah**-bay ...* un delito mayor / grave ...
a misdemeanor ...	*oon day-**lee**-toh may-**nohr** ...* un delito menor ...
a crime ...	*oon day-**lee**-toh ...* un delito ... [1]
a capital crime ...	*oon **kree**-mayn ...* un crimen ... [1]
3. ... according to ...	*... say-**goon** ...* ... según ...
state law.	*lah lay^ee ay-stah-**tahl**.* la ley estatal.
federal law.	*lah lay^ee fay-day-**rahl**.* la ley federal.
4. You are accused of ...	*lay ah-**koo**-sahn day ...* Le acusan de ...
(premeditated) murder.	*oh-mee-**see**-dee^oh / ah-say-see-**nah**-toh (pray-may-dee-**tah**-doh).* homicidio / asesinato (premeditado).
attempted murder.	*oh-moh-**see**-dee^oh froo-**strah**-doh.* homicidio frustrado.

aggravated assault.

*ah-gray-**see**^ohn ah-grah-**bah**-dah.*
agresión agravada.

sexual assault (of a minor).

*ah-gray-**see**^ohn sayk-**soo**^ahl (**kohn**-trah oon may-**nohr**).*
agresión sexual (contra un menor).

attempted sexual assault.

*ah-gray-**see**^ohn sayk-**soo**^ahl froo-**strah**-dah.*
agresión sexual frustrada.

(child) molestation.

*ah-**boo**-sohs days-oh-**nay**-stohs (day may-**noh**-rays).*
abusos deshonestos (de menores).

child abuse.

*ah-**boo**-soh day may-**noh**-rays.*
abuso de menores.

(attempted) rape.

*bee^oh-lah-**see**^ohn (froo-**strah**-dah).*
violación (frustrada.)

statutory rape.

*ay-**stoo**-proh.*
estupro.

arson.

*een-**sayn**-dee^oh een-tayn-see^oh-**nahl**.*
incendio intencional.

(attempted) kidnapping of a child.

*soo-strahk-**see**^ohn day may-**noh**-rays (froo-**strah**-dah).*
sustracción de menores (frustrada).

(armed) robbery.

*rroh-boh (ah **mah**-noh ahr-**mah**-dah).*
robo (a mano armada).

attempted robbery.

*rroh-boh froo-**strah**-doh.*
robo frustrado.

attempted armed robbery.

*rroh-boh ah **mah**-noh ahr-**mah**-dah froo-**strah**-doh.*
robo a mano armada frustrado.

assault and battery.

*ah-gray-**see**^ohn kohn lay-**see**^oh-nays.*
agresión con lesiones.

vehicular theft.

*rroh-boh bay-ee-koo-**lahr**.*
robo vehicular.

larceny.

*lah-troh-**see**-nee^oh.*
latrocinio.

burglary.

*rroh-boh kohn ah-yah-nah-**mee**^ayn-toh day moh-**rah**-dah/kohn ay-**skah**-loh.*
robo con allanamiento de morada / con escalo.

embezzlement.

*mahl-bayr-sah-**see**^ohn day **fohn**-dohs / days-**fahl**-koh.*
malversación de fondos / desfalco.

shoplifting.

*rroh-boh ayn lahs **tee**^ayn-dahs.*
robo en las tiendas.

fraud.

*frah^oo-day / ay-**stah**-fah.*
fraude / estafa.

drunkenness and disorderly conduct.	*kohn-**dook**-tah day boh-**rrah**-choh ee ahl-boh-roh-tah-**dohr**.* conducta de borracho y alborotador.
disorderly conduct.	*kohn-**dook**-tah ay-skahn-dah-**loh**-sah.* conducta escandalosa.
driving under the influence of . alcohol.	*mah-nay-**hahr** / kohn-doo-**seer** ayn ay-**stah**-doh day aym-bree^ah-**gays**.* manejar / conducir en estado de embriaguez.
driving while intoxicated.	*mah-nay-**hahr** / kohn-doo-**seer** bah-hoh lohs ay-**fayk**-tohs day* manejar / conducir bajo los efectos de
[meaning "drugs and alcohol"]	***droh**-gahs ee ahl-koh-**ohl**.* drogas y alcohol.
buying and selling illegal substances.	*bayn-**dayr** ee dis-tree-**boo^eer** soo-**stahn**-see^ahs ee-lay-**gah**-lays.* vender y distribuir sustancias ilegales.
falsifying (government) documents.	*fahl-see-fee-**kahr** doh-koo-**mayn**-tohs (goo-bayr-nah-mayn-**tah**-lays).* falsificar documentos (gubernamentales).
illegally carrying a fire arm.	*pohr-**tahr** oon **ahr**-mah day **foo^ay**-goh ee-lay-gahl-**mayn**-tay.* portar un arma de fuego ilegalmente.
prostitution.	*proh-stee-too-**see^ohn**.* prostitución.
driving a vehicle with	*mah-nay-**hahr** / kohn-doo-**seer** oon bay-ee-koo-loh kohn* manejar / conducir un vehículo con
a suspended / revoked license.	***oo**-nah lee-**sayn**-see^ah soo-spayn-**dee**-day / rray-boh-**kah**-dah.* una licencia suspendida / revocada.
narcotics / drug possession.	*poh-say-**see^ohn** day ay-stoo-pay-fah-**see^ayn**-tays / **droh**-gahs.* posesión de estupefacientes / drogas.
cannabis cultivation.	*kool-tee-**bahr** kah-**nah**-bees.* cultivar canabis.
grand theft.	***rroh**-boh mah-**yohr**.* robo mayor.
petty theft.	***rroh**-boh may-**nohr**.* robo menor.
treason.	*trah^ee-**see^ohn**.* traición.
espionage.	*ay-spee^oh-**nah**-hay.* espionaje.
racketeering.	***kree**-mayn ohr-gah-nee-**sah**-doh.* crimen organizado.
blackmail.	*chahn-**tah**-hay.* chantaje.

bribery.

*soh-**bohr**-noh.*
soborno.

trespass.

*ayn-**trah**-dah ee-lay-**gahl** ayn pro-pee^ay-**dahd** ah-**hay**-nah.*
entrada ilegal en propiedad ajena.

vandalism.

*bahn-dahl-**lees**-moh.*
vandalismo.

resisting arrest.

*rray-see-**stayn**-see^ah ah lah ah^oo-toh-ree-**dahd**.*
resistencia a la autoridad.

credit / debit card fraud.

***frah^oo**-day kohn tahr-**hay**-tah day **kray**-dee-toh / **day**-bee-toh.*
fraude con tarjeta de crédito / débito.

selling alcohol / tobacco to a minor.

*bayn-**dayr**-lay ahl-koh-**ohl** / tah-**bah**-koh ah oon may-**nohr**.*
venderle alcohol / tabaco a un menor.

buying alcohol / tobacco for a minor.

*kohm-**prahr** ahl-koh-**ohl** / tah-**bah**-koh **pah**-rah oon may-**nohr**.*
comprar alcohol / tabaco para un menor.

contributing to the delinquency
of a minor.

*kohn-tree-**boo^eer** ah lah day-leen-**koo^ayn**-see^ah day oon may-**nohr**.*
contribuir a la delincuencia de un menor.

possession of drug paraphernalia.

*poh-say-**see^ohn** day pah-rah-fayr-**nah**-lee^ah day **droh**-gahs.*
posesión de parafernalia de drogas.

violating parole/probation.

*bee^oh-**lahr** lah lee-bayr-**tahd** kohn-dee-see^oh-**nahl**/bee-hee-**lah**-dah.*
violar la libertad condicional/vigilada.

violating a restraining order.

*een-freen-**heer** oon **hoo^ee**-see^oh day ahm-**pah**-roh /*
infringir un juicio de amparo /

*/ **oo**-nah **ohr**-dayn een-ee-bee-**toh**-ree^ah.*
una orden inhibitoria.

domestic violence.

*bee^oh-**layn**-see^ah doh-**may**-stee-kah.*
violencia doméstica.

6. This is considered ...

*say kohn-see-**day**-rah **ay**-stoh ...*
Se considera esto ...

a felony ...

*oon day-**lee**-toh mah-**yohr** / **grah**-bay ...*
un delito mayor / grave ...

a misdemeanor ...

*oon day-**lee**-toh may-**nohr** ...*
un delito menor ...

a capital crime ...

*oon **kree**-mayn ...*
un crimen ... [1]

7. I am placing you under arrest.

*lay ay-**stoh^ee** ah-rray-**stahn**-doh.*
Le estoy arrestando.

8. I am taking you to jail.

*lay ay-**stoh^ee** yay-**bahn**-doh ah lah **kahr**-sayl.*
Le estoy llevando a la cárcel.

9. I am going to book you.	*lay boh^ee ah fee-**chahr**.* Le voy a fichar.
10. You are allowed — phone call(s).	*lay payr-**mee**-tayn — yah-**mah**-dah(s) tay-lay-**foh**-nee-kah(s).* Le permiten — llamada(s) telefónica(s). [3]

Notes

[1] The word *crimen (**kree**-mayn)* should only be used when speaking of a capital crime such a murder. Otherwise, the general term for *crime* is *delito*.

[2] Also, the term *secuestro de menores (frustrado) [say-**koo**^ay-stroh day may-**noh**-rays (froo-**strah**-doh)]* is interchangeable with *sustracción de menores (frustrada)*. The word *secuestro* can be a *hijacking* as well.

[3] If you wish to state only *one phone call,* use the word *una (**oo**-nah)* and the singular form *llamada*.

Practical Activities

Misdemeanors and Felonies

A) Oral Practice

Instructions: As you read in the **Notes** from the previous section, the way in which you address a *juvenile/minor* is different than how you speak to an *adult*. Understanding this difference is important so as not to sound comedic when addressing a *juvenile/minor* as if he/she were an *adult*. The differences are subtle, but nonetheless essential. In this oral practice, you will be asked to address a *juvenile/minor* directly and then address an *adult* with most of the same information. Make sure to make the distinctions based on the English phrases/expressions given in the first two sections of this chapter as well as previous chapters to help you. Afterwards, compare the Spanish phrases used to address the *juvenile/minor* with those used to address the *adult* and apply what you read in the **Notes** from the previous section, to point out how they differ.

I. Juvenile/Minor	**II. Adult**
1. You have broken the law.	1. You have broken the law.
2. You have committed a misdemeanor.	2. You have committed a felony according to federal law.
3. I am going to arrest you and I am sending you to a detention facility.	3. I am going to arrest you and I am taking you to jail.
4. You are allowed 2 phone calls.	4. You are allowed 1 phone call.
5. I am going to take you to the county jail for processing.	5. I am going to take you to the county jail for processing.
6. Be quiet, sit down and be still.	6. Be quiet, sit down and be still.
7. Cooperate fully.	7. Cooperate fully.
8. I am going to read you your rights.	8. I am going to read you your rights.

B) Juvenile or Adult?

Instructions: Decide if a *juvenile* or an *adult* is being addressed by writing **J** for *juvenile* or **A** for *adult* in the blank beside the number of each phrase/expression. You may want to reference past chapters if necessary.

1. __ Has cometido un delito.

2. __ Le voy a arrestar.

3. __ ¿Hablas un poco de inglés?

4. __ Cálmese.

5. __ Le voy a leer sus derechos.

6. __ Le acusan de estupro.

7. __ Te voy a arrestar.

8. __ Voy a ayudarle.

9. __ Coopera completamente.

10. __ Cálmate.

Follow-up

Instructions: After deciding which phrases/expressions are addressing a *juvenile* or an *adult*, discuss as a class how they differ. Are these changes very significant in structure? Point out clues you can use to distinguish phrases/expressions directed toward a *juvenile* from those said to an *adult*.

Cyber-Investigation

In the **Cyber-Investigation** from the previous section, you learned about the challenges many youths face that contribute greatly to juvenile delinquency. You were asked to focus on Hispanic youth and investigate how the factors that influence their behavior differ from those of other peer groups. This time, you are going to search for information regarding the difficulties Hispanic adults face when immigrating to a new country and how the immigration experience may adversely affect their behavior. Once you find this information, contrast it with that of already culturally assimilated Hispanics and describe how, if at all, their challenges differ.

Bookings and Releases

Before You Begin

Hispanics, along with other racial minorities, are disproportionately targeted and victimized by police and other law enforcement agents. This unequal targeting of minorities has given way to large minority prison populations, primarily consisting of Hispanic and black males. Inversely, this seriously impacts the view of minority populations and perpetuates their distrust in law enforcement and the legal system as a whole. Distrust among Hispanics is also heightened due to racial profiling associated with illegal immigration. In some instances, Hispanics suspected of being illegal have been brutalized by authorities without provocation.

Phrases

English	Pronunciation & Spanish
1. I am —.	*soh^ee* —. Soy —. [1]
2. This is the …	*ay*-stah ays … Esta es …
the county jail.	*lah kahr*-sayl dayl kohn-**dah**-doh. la cárcel del condado.
the local police station.	*lah koh-mee-sah-**ree**-ah loh-**kahl**. la comisaría local.
the county sheriff's office.	*lah oh-fee-**see**-nah dayl ahl-goo^ah-**seel** dayl kohn-**dah**-doh. la oficina del alguacil del condado.
3. You are in (proper name of location).	*ay-**stah** ayn (proper name of location).* Está en (proper name of location).
4. This is the address and	*ah-**kee** lay **tayn**-goh lah dee-rayk-**see^ohn** ee* Aquí le tengo la dirección y
telephone number.	*ayl **noo**-may-roh day tay-**lay**-foh-noh.* el número de teléfono.
5. Come with me.	*bayn*-gah kohn-**mee**-goh. Venga conmigo.
6. I need to take your picture.	*nay-say-**see**-tah sah-**kahr**-lay lah **foh**-toh.* Necesito sacarle la foto.
7. Stand here and face the camera.	***pohn**-gah-say ah-**kee** ee **mee**-ray lah **kah**-mah-rah.* Póngase aquí y mire la cámara.
8. Turn to the left.	*day **oo**-nah **koo^ahr**-tah **boo^ayl**-tah ah lah ees-**kee^ayr**-dah.* Dé una cuarta vuelta a la izquierda.

9. Turn forward.

*day **oo**-nah **koo^ahr**-tah **boo^ayl**-tah **ah**-see^ah day-**lahn**-tay.*
Dé una cuarta vuelta hacia delante.

10. Turn to the right.

*day **oo**-nah **koo^ahr**-tah **boo^ayl**-tah ah lah day-**ray**-chah.*
Dé una cuarta vuelta a la derecha.

11. Don't move.

*noh say **moo^ay**-bah.*
No se mueva.

12. I need to take your fingerprints.

*nay-say-**see**-toh sah-**kahr**-lay lahs **oo^ay**-yahs dee-hee-**tah**-lays / dahk-tee-**lah**-rays.*
Necesito sacarle las huellas digitales / dactilares.

13. Give me your right/left hand.

***day**-may lah **mah**-noh day-**ray**-chah / ees-**kee^ayr**-dah.*
Déme la mano derecha / izquierda.

14. Relax your hand.

*rray-**lah**-hay lah **mah**-noh.*
Relaje la mano.

15. Place you right/left hand here.

***pohn**-gah lah **mah**-noh day-**ray**-chah / ees-**kee^ayr**-dah ah-**kee**.*
Ponga la mano derecha / izquierda aquí.

16. I need to do it again.

*nay-say-**see**-toh ah-**sayr**-loh **oh**-trah bays.*
Necesito hacerlo otra vez.

17. Clean your hands with this.

***leem**-pee^ay lahs **mah**-nohs kohn **ay**-stoh.*
Limpie las manos con esto.

18. Sign here verifying that these

*feer-may ah-**kee pah**-rah bay-ree-fee-**kahr** kay **ay**-stahs*
Firme aquí para verificar que estas

   are your fingerprints.

*sohn soos **oo^ay**-yahs dee-hee-**tah**-lays.*
son sus huellas digitales.

19. Keep this copy for yourself.

***goo^ahr**-day **ay**-stah **koh**-pee^ah **pah**-ray see **mees**-moh/mah.*
Guarde esta copia para sí mismo/a. [2]

20. You have been arrested for —.

*ah **see**-doh ah-rray-**stah**-doh/dah pohr —.*
Ha sido arrestado/a por —. [2]

21. Empty your pockets and place all your

*bah-**see**-ay lohs bohl-**see**-yohs ee **pohn**-gah **toh**-dahs soos*
Vacíe los bolsillos y ponga todas sus

   belongings in this.

*payr-tay-**nayn**-see^ahs ayn **ay**-stoh.*
pertenencias en esto.

22. Are you hiding anything on your person?

*ay-**stah** ay-skohn-**dee^ayn**-doh ahl-goh ayn soo payr-**soh**-nah?*
¿Está escondiendo algo en su persona?

23. I need ...

*nay-say-**see**-toh ...*
Necesito ...

   to search you.

*rray-hee-**strahr**-lay.*
registrarle.

   frisk you/pat you down.

*pal-**pahr**-lay.*
palparle.

24. Spit out whatever is in your mouth.

*ay-**skoo**-pah loh kay **tayn**-gah ayn lah **boh**-kah.*
Escupa lo que tenga en la boca.

25. Open your mouth and stick out your tongue.

*ah-brah lah **boh**-kah ee **sah**-kay lah **layn**-goo^ah.*
Abra la boca y saque la lengua.

26. Lift up …

*lay-**bahn**-tay …*
Levante …

your arms.

*lohs **brah**-sohs.*
los brazos.

your right / left breast.

*ayl **say**-noh day-**ray**-choh / ees-**kee**^ayr-doh.*
el seno derecho / izquierdo.

27. Show me the soles of your shoes.

*moo^**ay**-stray-may lahs **soo**^ay-lahs day lohs sah-**pah**-tohs.*
Muéstreme las suelas de los zapatos.

28. I need to do a strip search.

*nay-say-**see**-toh ah-**sayr**-lay oon rray-**hee**-stroh ahl days-**noo**-doh.*
Necesito hacerle un registro al desnudo.

29. Remove all of your clothing.

*days-**noo**-day-say pohr kohm-**play**-toh.*
Desnúdese por completo.

30. Bend over and spread your buttocks

*een-**klee**-nay-say ee say-**pah**-ray lahs **nahl**-gahs*
Inclínese y separe las nalgas

with your fingers.

*kohn lohs **day**-dohs.*
con los dedos.

31. Take out your tampon and place it

*sah-kay ayl tahm-**pohn** ee **pohn**-gah-loh*
Saque el tampón y póngalo

in here.

*ayn **ay**-stoh.*
en esto.

32. I'll give you another tampon.

*lay dah-**ray oh**-troh tahm-**pohn**.*
Le daré otro tampón.

33. You can get dressed now.

*poo^**ay**-day poh-**nayr**-say lah **rroh**-pah ah-**oh**-rah.*
Puede ponerse la ropa ahora.

34. I will put this with your belongings.

*pohn-**dray ay**-stoh kohn soos payr-tay-**nayn**-see^ahs.*
Pondré esto con sus pertenencias.

35. Your belongings will be returned to you

*say lay day-bohl-bayr-**rahn** soos payr-tay-**nayn**-see^ahs*
Se le devolverán sus pertenencias

upon your release.

*ahl sayr lee-**brah**-doh/dah.*
al ser librado/a.[3]

36. I going to put you in a

*boh^ee ah poh-**nayr**-lay ayn **oo**-nah*
Voy a ponerle en una

temporary holding cell.

*s**ayl**-dah day day-tayn-**see**^ohn taym-poh-**rahl**.*
celda de detención temporal.

37. I'll let you know when your family gets here.

*lay day-hah-**ray** sah-**bayr** koo^ahn-doh **yay**-gay soo fah-**mee**-lee^ah.*
Le dejaré saber cuando llegue su familia.[4]

38. Your bail has been set at — dollars.

*ahn fee-**hah**-doh soo **fee^ahn**-sah ah -—**doh**-lah-rays.*
Han fijado su fianza a — dólares. [4]

39. You will have to pay (a portion of) the bail/bond

*tayn-**drah** kay pah-**gahr** (**oo**-nah **pahr**-tay day) lah **fee^ahn**-sah*
Tendrá que pagar (una parte de) la fianza

to get out on bail/bond.

*pah-**rah** sayr lee-bay-**rah**-doh/dah **bah**-hoh **fee^ahn**-sah.*
para ser liberado/a bajo fianza.[5]

40. The bail/bond is not a fine.

*lah **fee^ahn**-sah noh ays **oo**-nah **mool**-tah.*
La fianza no es una multa.

41. Paying a bond/bail is a way of

*say ayn-**tray**-gah **oo**-nah **fee^ahn**-sah **koh**-moh **fohr**-mah day*
Se entrega una fianza como forma de

guaranteeing that …

*gah-rahn-tee-**sahr** kay …*
garantizar que …

a person is not going to

*oo-nah payr-**soh**-nah noh bah ah kay-brahn-**tahr** lah lee-bayr-**tahd***
una persona no va a quebrantar la libertad

jump bail.

*bah-hoh **fee^ahn**-sah.*
bajo fianza.

a person is not going to flee before

*oo-nah payr-**soh**-nah noh bah ah oo^eer **ahn**-tays*
una persona no va a huir antes

having to appear before the judge.

*day tay-**nayr** kay kohm-pah-ray-**sayr** **ahn**-tay ayl hoo^ays.*
de tener que comparecer ante el juez.

42. You can look in the phone book

*poo^**ay**-day kohn-sool-**tahr** lah **ghee**-ah tay-lay-**foh**-nee-kah*
Puede consultar la guía telefónica

for a listing of bailbondsmen.

*pah-**rah** **oo**-nah **lee**-stah day fee^ah-**doh**-rays.*
para una lista de fiadores.

43. You are free to go.

*ay-**stah** **lee**-bray **pah**-rah **eer**-say.*
Está libre para irse.

44. We are releasing you.

*lay ay-**stah**-mohs lee-bay-**rahn**-doh.*
Le estamos liberando.

45. Sign here indicating you have

*feer-may ah-**kee** **pah**-rah een-dee-**kahr** kay ah*
Firme aquí para indicar que ha

received your belongings.

*rray-see-**bee**-doh soos payr-tay-**nayn**-see^ahs.*
recibido sus pertenencias.

46. This document explains why you were arrested.

*ay-stay doh-koo-**mayn**-toh ayk-**splee**-kah pohr kay lay ah-rray-**stah**-rohn.*
Este documento explica por qué le arrestaron.

47. This is documentation of your booking.

*ay-stah ays doh-koo-mayn-tah-**see^ohn** day soo day-tayn-**see^ohn**.*
Esta es documentación de su detención.

48. This is the date and time you must

*ayh-stahs sohn lah **fay**-chah ee lah **oh**-rah kay ah day*
Estas son la fecha y la hora que ha de

appear before the court/judge.

*kohm-pah-ray-**sayr ahn**-tay ayl tree-boo-**nahl** / hoo^ays.*
comparecer ante el tribunal / juez.

49. This is your booking number.

*ay-stay ays soo **noo**-may-roh day day-tayn-**see^ohn** poh-lee-**see^ahl**.*
Este es su número de detención policial.

50. This is the name and contact information

*ay-stohs sohn ayl **nohm**-bray ee lah een-fohr-mah-**see^ohn** day kohn-**tahk**-toh*
Estos son el nombre y la información de contacto

for your probation/parole officer.

*day soo ah-**hayn**-tay day lee-bayr-**tahd** kohn-dee-see^oh-**nahl** bee-hee-**lah**-dah.*
de su agente de libertad condicional/vigilada.

51. You should contact him / her as soon
as possible.

***day**-bay koh-moo-nee-**kahr**-say kohn ayl / **ay**-yah ayn say-**ghee**-dah.*
Debe comunicarse con él / ella en seguida.

52. He/She will explain what happens next.

*lay ayk-splee-kah-**rah** loh kay pah-sah-**rah** ah kohn-tee-noo^ah-**see^ohn**.*
Le explicará lo que pasará a continuación.

53. This is the location of your vehicle.

*ay-stah ays lah loh-kah-lee-sah-**see^ohn** day soo bay-**ee**-koo-loh.*
Esta es la localización de su vehículo.

54. Your vehicle is at an impound yard.

*soo bay-**ee**-koo-loh ay-**stah** ayn oon day-**poh**-see-toh day bay-**ee**-koo-lohs.*
Su vehículo está en un depósito de vehículos. [6]

55. Call this number to retrieve it.

***yah**-may ah **ay**-stay **noo**-may-roh **pah**-rah rray-koo-pay-**rahr**-loh.*
Llame a este número para recuperarlo.

56. You will have to pay the impound fees

*tayn-**drah** kay pah-**gahr** lohs day-**ray**-chohs day ahl-mah-say-**nah**-hay*
Tendrá que pagar los derechos de almacenaje

to get your vehicle.

***pah**-rah rray-koo-pay-**rahr** soo bay-**ee**-koo-loh.*
para recuperar su vehículo.

57. Your vehicle is parked outside.

*soo bay-**ee**-koo-loh ay-**stah** ay-stah-see^oh-**nah**-doh ah-**foo^ay**-rah.*
Su vehículo está estacionado afuera.

Notes

[1] Identify yourself with the proper title from *Chapter 1 - Identifying Yourself* and *Preliminary Scene Assessment* where appropriate. You may also want to reference past chapters especially *Chapter 2 - Multipurpose Interview for Personal Data and Information.*

[2] See *Chapter 11 - Misdemeanors and Felonies.*

[3] Use the *–o* ending when speaking to a *male* and the *–a* ending when speaking to a *female.*

[4] Write the number down for the individual instead of saying it. When working with larger numbers this will help avoid miscommunication.

[5] See *Chapter 15 - Family and Friends* for useful vocabulary.

[6] Also, used for an impound yard is *un corralón (oon koh-rrah-**lohn**).*

Practical Activities

Bookings and Releases

A) Oral Practice

Instructions: Prepare what you will say to a Spanish-speaker in order to obtain the required information or carry out the following tasks. Reference previous sections if necessary. Use a minimum of four phrases/expressions in your communiqué. Once you have finished, find a partner and practice with each other. Ask you partner to try and understand what you say without having to consult the text.

1. Take a suspect's/inmate's picture.
2. Obtain a suspect's/inmate's finger prints.
3. Perform a search of the suspect/inmate.
4. Perform an oral cavity search.
5. Perform a strip-search of a male suspect/inmate.
6. Perform a strip-search of a female suspect/inmate.
7. Explain a bond, how much the bond is and where to obtain a bondsman.
8. Return the suspect's belongings and explain how to retrieve his/her vehicle.

B) Translation

Instructions: Translate into English what this public safety official is saying to a Spanish-speaking suspect and his spouse. Attempt to translate as much of the information as possible without looking back in this section. If you get stuck, consult a classmate. After you have finished, form groups of 3 to 4 members and review your oral or written translations together and make any necessary corrections at that time.

Al sospechoso:

Soy el agente Rodríguez. Esta es la comisaría local. Aquí le tengo la dirección y el número de teléfono. Le permiten una llamada. ¿Quisiera hacer una llamada? ... Venga conmigo. Necesito sacarle la foto y las huellas digitales.... Firme aquí para verificar que estas son sus huellas digitales.... Necesito palparle.... Levante los brazos.... Muéstreme las suelas de los zapatos. Voy a ponerle en una celda de detención temporal. Le dejaré saber cuando llegue su esposa.

A la esposa:

Han fijado su fianza a 2.500 dólares. Tendrá que pagar una parte de la fianza para ser librado. Se entrega una fianza como una forma de garantizar que una persona no va a huir antes de tener que comparecer ante el juez. No es una multa. Puede consultar la guía telefónica para una lista de fiadores.

Al sospechoso:

Está libre para irse. Este documento le explica por qué le arrestaron. Estos son el nombre y la información de contacto de su agente de libertad vigilada. Debe comunicarse con ella en seguida. Le explicará lo que pasará a continuación. Habla español.

Chapter 12

Hispanic Gang Related Slang[1]

Before You Begin

Generally, Hispanic gangs are not lead by one leader but rather by a group of leaders; each one possessing some specific ability. For example, a gang wishing to plan an attack on a rival gang may call upon the member from this group of leaders with the most fighting experience to coordinate the event. Today's Hispanic street gangs have a "prison mentality" meaning they follow the ideal that *you are entitled to whatever you want* and that *if someone insults you or makes you angry, they deserve to die.* Hispanic gang members are loyal until death and are proud of their gang membership. Hispanic gangs may be one unit but function as several different "cliques." These are subsets of the primary gang unit whose members are peers and live within certain areas of the gang's territory. The protection of this territory, or *turf (in Spanish, barrio [**bah**-rree^oh]),* from not only rival gangs but government agencies as well, is of the utmost importance for the gang and it's members.

The manner in which a Hispanic gang member dresses serves to identify the individual by the gang to which he or she belongs. Standard dress is easy to recognize and most often consists of oversized khaki pants or jeans, cut up the sides above each ankle, athletic shoes, mostly white, or highly polished leather shoes, oversized t-shirts and/or button-down collar dress shirts and a bandanna or baseball cap. The oversize clothing allows for easy concealment of weapons, etc. Likewise, tattoos will include gang symbols, names and/or initials of other members, especially those that have been killed.

Phrases

English	Pronunciation & Spanish
1. Chicano slang; Mexican slang	*kah-**loh**; pah-**choo**-koh* caló; pachuco
2. For life. [found in graffiti and tattoos; means a gang member is a member for life]	*pohr **bee**-dah.* Por vida. [2]
3. My crazy life. [living for the moment regardless of the consequences]	*mee **bee**-dah **loh**-kah.* Mi vida loca.
4. With safety. [written under graffiti as warning not to deface or else]	*kohn **sah**-fohs.* Con safos. [3]
5. Live to kill.	*bee-**beer pah**-rah mah-**tahr**.* Vivir para matar.

6. Hey dude/man!	*ay-say **bah**-toh!* ¡Ese vato!
7. Stay alert!	***troo**-chah!* ¡Trucha!
8. Don't chicken out!	*noh tay **rrah**-hahs!* ¡No te rajas!
9. Until death!	***ah**-stah lah **moo^ayr**-tay!* ¡Hasta la muerte!
10. (You) / He / She is afraid.	*ay-**stah(s)** ay-skah-**mah**-doh/dah.* Está(s) escamado/a. ⁴
11. (You) / He / She is angry, mad.	*ay-**stah(s)** ah-way-**tah**-doh/dah.* Está(s) awetado/a.⁴
12. We rule.	*rree-**fah**-mohs.* Rifamos. ⁵
13. We control.	*kohn-troh-**lah**-mohs.* Controlamos.
14. Excuse me.	*day-**spayn**-sah.* Despensa.
15. All right!; Hey man!	***oh**-rah-lay!* ¡Orale!
16. We're new. So what's it to you?	***noo^ay**-boh. ee kay?* Nuevo. ¿Y qué? [often found in graffiti]
17. What a bummer, bad scene!	*kay **gah**-choh!* ¡Qué gacho!
18. It's over!; That's it!	*yah **stoo**-boh!* ¡Ya stuvo!
19. So what? [used a a challenge]	*ee kay?* ¿Y qué?
20. Bullshit!	***poo**-rah **kah**-kah!; **pay**-droh!* ¡Pura caca!; ¡Pedro!
21. (You) / He / She was arrested.	*(**foo^ee**-stay) foo^ay tohr-**see**-doh/dah.* (Fuiste) Fue torcido/a. ⁶
22. male cousin	***pree**-moh* primo ⁷
23. MS-13	***mah**-rah sahl-bah-**troo**-chah* Mara Salvatrucha ⁸
24. Mara Salvatrucha [gang member]	*mah-**ray**-roh* marero

25. gang	*bahn-dah; pahn-dee-yah* banda; pandilla	
26. gang member	*pahn-dee-yay-roh/rah* pandillero/a [9]	
27. he	*ayl, lohs* EL, LOS [10]	
28. she	*lah, lahs* LA, LAS [10]	
29. male/female gangster	*choh-loh/lah* cholo/a [9,11]	
30. young male/female gangster [may indicate a want-to-be gang member]	*cho-lee-toh/tah* cholito/a [9,11]	
31. set, clique, posse	*klee-kah* clica, clika OR klika	
32. man, boy, dude	*bah-toh* vato	
33. crazy dudes/guys	*bah-tohs loh-kohs* vatos locos [12]	
34. crazy dude	*bah-toh loh-koh* vato loco [13]	
35. hood (neighborhood), turf	*bah-rree^oh* barrio OR varrio [14]	
36. local thieves	*kah-kohs* cacos	
37. brother(s) [in the figurative sense]	*kahr-nahl(-es)* carnal(es)	
38. sister(s) [in the figurative sense]	*kahr-nah-lah(s)* carnala(s)	
39. Indian warrior	*chah-kah* chaca	
40. warrior	*gay-rray-roh/rah* guerrero/a [9]	
41. homeboy, homie	*ay-say* ese [15]	
42. leader	*ayl pree-mayr pah-lah-brah* el primer palabra	
43. chunts, "Mexican nationals"; wetbacks [derogatory]	*choon-tah-rohs; moh-hah-dohs* chúntaros; mojados [16]	

44. Mexican American	*poh*-choh pocho [16]
45. girls	*hah^ee*-nahs jainas
46. anglos, whites	gah-***bah***-chohs; ***gah***-bahs; ***goo^ay***-rohs; ***sah***-bah-nahs gabachos; gabas; güeros; sábanas[16]
47. anglicized	ayn-gah-bah-chay-***ah***-doh/dah engabacheado/a
48. African Americans, blacks	mah^ee-***yah***-tays; ***teen***-tohs; chah-***nah***-tays; mayates; tintos; chanates; ***pee***-nahs; tay-***roh***-nays [16] pinas; terones
49. police	***choh***-tah; lah lay^ee chota; la ley
50. police officer, pig	mah-***rrah***-noh marrano
51. lady, gang girl	***rroo***-kah ruka, ruca
52. veteran gang member	bay-tay-***rah***-noh; ***choo***-koh veterano; chuco
53. friend, associate	kah-mah-***rah***-dah camarada
54. kiss ass, brown-noser	lahm-***bee^ohn*** lambión
55. sell-out, snitch	bayn-***dee***-doh vendido
56. lesbian	***hoh***-tah jota [16]
57. homosexual	***hoh***-toh; mah-ree-***kohn*** joto; maricón [16]
58. homie	koo^***ah***-tay cuate
59. ex-convict, state prisoner	***peen***-toh pinto
60. idiot	***mayn***-soh menso
61. pest	***moh***-skah; ***moh***-sah mosca; mosa

62. rat, snitch	*rrah-tah; rray-**lah**-hay* rata; relaje
63. dress suit [actual word for "zootsuit"]	*pah-**choo**-koh* pachuco
64. outfit	*rree^ah-tah; pee-**see**^oh-lah* riata; pisiola
65. shirt	***lee**-sah* lisa
66. bandanna	***moh**-koh rrahg* moco rag
67. hands	*bah^**ee**-sahs* vaisas
68. shoes	***kahr**-kohs* carcos
69. house	*kahn-**tohn*** cantón
70. fight	***pay**-doh* pedo
71. trouble	***play**^ee-toh* pleito
72. "dance" [used to start a fight]	***bay**^ee-lay* baile
73. county jail	*ayl kohn-**dah**-dah* el condada
74. job, work	*ayl **hah**-lay; lah **cheen**-gah* el jale; la chinga [swear word]
75. gun; firearm	*koo^**ay**-tay* cuete
76. gang initiation	***sahl**-toh; ayn **sahl**-toh* salto; en salto
77. blows, fighting	*cheen-**gah**-sohs* chingazos [swear word]
78. tags, gang markings	***plah**-kahs* placas
79. police badge	***plah**-kah* placa
80. rules and regulations of Hispanic gangs	*moh-**bee**-dahs* movidas

81. high, drunk or crazy acting	*loh-**koh**-tay* locote
82. act of agression or violence	*loh-**koo**-rah* locura
83. to get out, leave	*skoo^ayn-**tahr*** squentar
84. to eat	*rray-fee-**nahr*** refinar
85. food	***rray**-feen; pay-**pee**-reen* refin; pepirin
86. to smoke	*choo-**pahr**; doh-**rahr*** chupar; dorar [17]
87. to drink alcohol	*pee-**stee**^ahr* pistiar
88. hard liquor	*peest* pist
89. small bag	*boh-**rray**-goh* borrego
90. drug needle	***klah**-boh; **poon**-tah; ah-**goo**-hah* clavo; punta; aguja
91. drugs	***kah**-kah* caca [swear word]
92. heroin	***kahr**-gah; **chee**-bah; **ah**-chay* carga: chiva; hache [18]
93. marijuana	***yay**-skah; **gree**-fah; **rree**-fah; **moh**-tah; ee^**ayr**-bah* yesca; grifa; rifa; mota; yierba
94. crack cocaine	***doo**-rah* dura
95. cocaine	***tahl**-koh* talco
96. heroin user	*tay-**kah**-toh/tah* tecato/a [9]
97. cigarettes	***frah**-hohs* frajos
98. bonded, united; good, straight person	***feer**-may* firme
99. jail	***boh**-tay; **tahn**-kay* bote; tanque

100. asshole	*koo-**lay**-roh* culero/a [9]
101. car	*kah-**rroo**-chah;* ***rrahn**-flah* carrucha; ranfla
102. beat-up old car	*kahr-**kahn**-chah* carcancha
103. knife	***fee**-lah; fee-**lay**-roh* fila; filero
104. silent treatment	***lay**-bah* leva
105. penitentiary	***peen**-tah* pinta
106. Mexican Mafia	[represented by the letter -M- or the number -13- in graffiti]
107. "Our family" [referring to gang as a family unit]	***noo^ay**-strah fah-**mee**-lee^ah* "Nuestra Familia" - [represented by the letters -NF- in graffiti]
108. Northern California Gang/Norte Califas	[represented by the letter -N- or the number -14 - in graffiti X3 or TRECE]
109. Southern California Gang/Southern Califas	[represented by -13 Sur- in graffiti]

Notes

[1] No practical activities are provided for this section since it is strictly informational. However, practicing the terms aloud, listening to their pronunciation and studying their meaning is highly suggested so as to be aware of these terms and expressions when you hear or possibly see them. However, due to the nature of this topic, a **CYBER-INVESTIGATION** has been provided and is highly suggested.

[2] Also written as *P/V* in tattoos and graffiti.

[3] Also written as *C/S* in graffiti.

[4] The *está* form would be used for *he/she* and the *estás* form would be used for *informal you*. Also, the *-o* ending would refer to *males* and the *-a* ending to *females*.

[5] Also appears in graffiti as *-R-*.

[6] The *fue* form would be used for *he/she* and the *fuiste* form would be used for *informal you*. Also, the *-o* ending would refer to *males* and the *-a* ending to *females*.

[7] In gang slang, this is a marijuana joint laced with cocaine

[8] Mara Salvatrucha (MS-13 or MS) is a powerful Central American gang founded in Los Angeles in 1980 by Salvadoran immigrants. The gang operates mainly in Central America and the U.S., but there are traces of the gang in Canada and South America as well. The gang was initially formed to protect Salvadoran immigrants from the Mexican rival gangs that would prey on them.

[9] The *-o* ending would refer to *males* and the *-a* ending to *females*.

[10] Appears in graffiti to identify the gender of the gang.

[11] May be derogatory when used by non-gang members.

[12] Also appears as -L's- in graffiti.

[13] Also appears as -L- in graffiti.

[14] Also appears as -B- or -V- in graffiti.

[15] May be considered derogatory if said by a non-Hispanic.

[16] Depending on context and circumstance, these terms may be viewed as derogatory.

[17] The verb *dorar* can also mean *to cook (as in drugs)*.

[18] Also represented by the number 8 meaning the 8th letter of the alphabet -H- as well as represented by the letter -H- itself.

Cyber-Investigation

Being able to decipher gang tattoos and gang graffiti may be very helpful in your respective profession. There is a lot of information on this topic on the Internet that you may find beneficial. Conduct a search for *Hispanic Gang Tattoos* and *Hispanic Gang Graffiti* to see what you find. Share pertinent information with classmates and discuss how such information may assist you on the job or in you future career. Don't forget to check for images as well.

Chapter 13

Managing Phone Calls in Spanish

Phrases

English	Pronunciation & Spanish
1. (Hello), I am —.	*(oh-lah) soh^ee —.* (Hola) soy —. [1]
2. Do you speak (any) English?	*ah-blah (oon poh-koh day) een-glays?* ¿Habla (un poco de) inglés?
3. Do you understand (any) English?	*kohm-prayn-day (oon poh-koh day) een-glays?* ¿Comprende (un poco de) inglés?
4. I speak (a little) Spanish.	*ah-bloh (oon poh-koh day) ay-spahn-yohl.* Hablo (un poco de) español.
5. I understand (a little) Spanish.	*kohm-prayn-doh (oon poh-koh day) ay-spahn-yohl.* Comprendo (un poco de) español.
6. Please (calm down and) speak slower.	*pohr fah-bohr (kahl-may-say ee) ah-blay mahs day-spah-see^oh.* Por favor, (cálmese y) hable más despacio.
7. For whom are you calling?	*pah-rah kee^ayn yah-mah?* ¿Para quién llama?
8. I'm sorry, I don't understand (very well).	*loh see^ayn-toh noh kohm-prayn-doh (moo^ee bee^ayn).* Lo siento, no comprendo (muy bien).
9. Please hold.	*pohr fah-bohr noh koo^ayl-gay.* Por favor, no cuelgue.
10. I'm going to transfer the call to ...	*boh^ee ah pah-sahr lah yah-mah-dah con ...* Voy a pasar la llamada con ...
someone who speaks Spanish.	*ahl-ghee^ayn kay ah-blah ay-spahn-yohl.* alguien que habla español.
his/her secretary.	*soo say-kray-tah-ree^oh/ah.* su secretario/a. [2]
his/her receptionist.	*soo rray-sayp-see^oh-nee-stah.* su recepcionista.
his/her assistant.	*soo ah^ee-yoo-dahn-tay.* su ayudante.
his/her coworker.	*soo koh-lay-gah.* su colega.
someone else.	*oh-trah payr-soh-nah.* otra persona.

11. If no one answers, leave a message.	*see **nah**-dee^ay kohn-**tay**-stah **day**-hay oon mayn-**sah**-hay.* Si nadie contesta, deje un mensaje.
12. Speak clearly and slowly.	***ah**-blay **klah**-rah ee layn-tah-**mayn**-tay.* Hable clara y lentamente.
13. Leave your name, telephone number and	***day**-hay soo **nohm**-bray **noo**-may-roh day tay-**lay**-foh-noh ee* Deje su nombre, número de teléfono y
a brief message.	*oon **bray**-bay mayn-**sah**-hay.* un breve mensaje.
14. If this is an emergency, hang up and	*see **ay**-stah ays **oo**-nah ay-mayr-**hayn**-see^ah **koo^ayl**-gay ee* Si ésta es una emergencia, cuelgue y
dial 9-1-1.	***mahr**-kay ayl **noo^ay**-bay **oo**-noh **oo**-noh.* marque el 9 1 1.
15. With whom would you like to speak?	*kohn kee^ayn day-**say**-ah ah-**blahr**?* ¿Con quién desea hablar?
16. He/She is not available at this time.	*noh say ayn-**koo^ayn**-trah ayn **ay**-stay moh-**mayn**-toh.* No se encuentra en este momento.
17. I'm going to send your call to his/her voicemail.	*boh^ee ah pah-**sahr** lah yah-**mah**-dah kohn soo boo-**sohn** day bohs.* Voy a pasar la llamada con su buzón de voz.
18. Do you want me to take a message	***kee^ay**-ray kay **toh**-may oon mayn-**sah**-hay* ¿Quiere que tome un mensaje
and have someone call you back?	*ee **ah**-gah kay **ahl**-ghee^ayn lay **yah**-may?* y haga que alguien le llame?
19. What is your full name?	*koo^ahl ays soo **nohm**-bray kohm-**play**-toh?* ¿Cuál es su nombre completo?
20. How do you spell …	***koh**-moh say ay-**skree**-bay …* ¿Cómo se escribe …
your first name?	*soo pree-**mayr nohm**-bray?* su primer nombre?
your last name?	*soo ah-pay-**yee**-doh?* su apellido?
21. Slower, please.	*mahs day-**spah**-see^oh pohr fah-**bohr**.* Más despacio, por favor.
22. Repeat it, please.	*rray-**pee**-tah-loh pohr fah-**bohr**.* Repítalo, por favor.
23. What is your telephone number?	*koo^ahl ays soo **noo**-may-roh day tay-**lay**-foh-noh?* ¿Cuál es su número de teléfono?
24. Is this an urgent/pressing situation?	***ay**-stah ays **oo**-nah see-too^ah-**see^ohn** oor-**hayn**-tay?* ¿Esta es una situación urgente?

25. He/She is not here ...

*noh ay-**stah** ...*
No está ...

    today.

oh^ee.
hoy.

    this week.

*ay-stah say-**mah**-nah.*
esta semana.

26. He/She is on vacation.

*ay-**stah** day bah-kah-**see^oh**-nays.*
Está de vacaciones.

27. He/She does not work here (anymore).

*(yah) noh trah-**bah**-hah ah-**kee**.*
(Ya) no trabaja aquí.

28. You have the wrong number.

*say ah ay-kee-boh-**kah**-doh day **noo**-may-roh.*
Se ha equivocado de número.

29. You need to call this number, —.

*nay-say-**see**-tah yah-**mahr** ah **ay**-stay **noo**-may-roh—.*
Necesita llamar a este número, —.

30. Dial this extension, —.

*mahr-kay **ay**-stay **noo**-may-roh day ayk-stayn-**see^ohn**—.*
Marque este número de extensión, —.

31. Please call back ...

*pohr fah-**bohr yah**-may ...*
Por favor, llame ... ³

    later.

*mahs **tahr**-day.*
más tarde.

    tomorrow.

*mahn-**yah**-nah.*
mañana.

    this afternoon.

*ay-stah **tahr**-day.*
esta tarde.

    this evening.

*ay-stah **noh**-chay.*
esta noche.

    tomorrow morning.

*mahn-**yah**-nah pohr lah mahn-**yah**-nah.*
mañana por la mañana.

    tomorrow afternoon.

*mahn-**yah**-nah pohr lah **tahr**-day.*
mañana por la tarde.

    tomorrow evening.

*mahn-**yah**-nah pohr lah **noh**-chay.*
mañana por la noche.

32. Thank you and have a nice day.

*grah-**see^ahs** ee kay **pah**-say oon boo^ayn **dee**-ah.*
Gracias y que pase un buen día.

33. I'm sorry I cannot help.

*see^**ayn**-toh noh poh-**dayr** ah^ee-yoo-**dahr**.*
Siento no poder ayudar.

34. There is no one here by that name.

*noh ah^ee **nah**-dee^ay ah-**kee** kohn **ay**-stay **nohm**-bray.*
No hay nadie aquí con este nombre.

35. Would you like to make an appointment	*kee-**see**^**ay**-rah ah-**sayr** oo-nah **see**-tah* ¿Quisiera hacer una cita	
to meet	***pah**-rah rray^oo-**neer**-say* para reunirse	
with him / her?	*kohn ayl / **ay**-yah?* con él / ella?	

36. There is an appointment available	*ah^ee **oo**-nah **see**-tah dee-spoh-**nee**-blay* Hay una cita disponible
on the—of—at—.	***pah**-rah ayl—day—ah lah / lahs—.* para el—de—a la / las—.[3]

37. Your appointment is on the—of—at—.	*soo **see**-tah ays ayl—day—ah lah / lahs—.* Su cita es el—de—a la / las—. [3]

38. Call this number if you need to cancel,	***yah**-may ah **ay**-stay **noo**-may-roh see nay-say-**see**-tah kahn-say-**lahr** oh* Llame a este número si necesita cancelar o
reschedule or cannot make it.	*rray-proh-grah-**mahr** lah **see**-tah oh see noh **poo**^**ay**-day bay-**neer**.* reprogramar la cita o si no puede venir.

Notes

[1] After you realize the caller is a Spanish speaker identify yourself with the proper title from *Chapter 1 - Identifying Yourself and Preliminary Scene Assessment* as appropriate. Also, there are many regional ways to answer a phone in Spanish, a simple *Hello (Hola)* will suffice here. It has been provided should you need to place a caller on hold and come back to him/her and verify he/she is still on line.

[2] If the *secretary* is *male* use the *-o ending*; if *female* use the *-a ending*.

[3] Also reference *Chapter 17 - Telling Time the Easy Ways* and *Chapter 17 - Telling Time the Easy Ways - Days, Months and Dates.*

Practical Activities

A) Oral Practice

Instructions: Speaking in a foreign language by phone is quite challenging. No body language or facial expressions are available to assist you in conveying your message or comprehending that of the speaker. Therefore, your pronunciation will be essential in your communication. Choose one of the scenarios below and prepare how you will handle that "phone call" in Spanish. After you have decided what you will say, practice aloud individually.

1. You answer the phone and realize the caller is Spanish-speaking. Find out for whom he/she is calling; request the caller to hold and you will transfer the call and that if no one answers, to please leave a message. Remind the caller to speak clearly and slowly.
2. A transferred call rings back to you and the speaker is talking too quickly. Have the caller slow down; find out with whom he/she would like to speak; state that person is not available and ask if he/she would like to leave a message with a name and phone number.
3. You are trying to take down a brief message from a caller whom you do not understand, state you don't speak Spanish well; get a name and phone number; state you do not understand and ask him/her to repeat the information slowly. Let the caller know you will have someone call him/her back.
4. A caller sounds frantic so you ask if the situation is urgent. He/she says yes. Ask with whom he/she would like to speak. You realize that person is not in today; give the caller an alternate number to call followed by the appropriate extension. Thank the caller and tell him/her to have a nice day.
5. You answer the phone and realize you are speaking with a Spanish-speaker talking very quickly. Ask the caller to slow down and repeat the information. You understand he/she has an appointment and needs to cancel and reschedule. Provide the caller with an alternate appointment date and time (which he/she accepts) then restate the date and time of the appointment. Thank the caller and say goodbye.

B) Matching Questions and Answers

Instructions: For phone calls, it will be somewhat important to be able to understand simple Spanish words and phrases said by callers. To help you prepare for this, match the Spanish questions below with the Spanish answer. After you have finished, compare your answer with those of a classmate. Finally, have your instructor review the correct responses and practice translating the question and the answer aloud in English.

1. ___ ¿Para quién llama?

a. Morales, M-O-R-A-L-E-S.

2. ___ ¿Con quién desea hablar?

b. Es el 555-9234.

3. ___ ¿Cuál es su nombre completo?

c. Sí, por favor. El lunes a las 2 de la tarde.

4. ___ ¿Cómo se escribe su apellido?

d. No, lo siento. Sólo español.

5. ___ ¿Esta es una situación urgente?

e. No, no es necesario. Llamo más tarde.

6. ___ ¿Quisiera hacer una cita para reunirse con él?

f. Samuel, S-A-M-U-E-L.

7 ___ ¿Quiere que tome un mensaje y haga que

    alguien le llame?

g. Para el señor Johnston.

8. ___ ¿Cuál es su número de teléfono?

h. Alvaro Torres.

9. ___ ¿Cómo se escribe su primer nombre?

i. Con la señorita McNeal.

10. ___ ¿Comprende un poco de inglés?

j. Sí, es importante.

Follow-Up

Instructions: Using the questions from this exercise, invent your own answers in Spanish. Then, form groups of three to four people and take turns reading these answers aloud. The group members will try to match the corresponding question to the answer they hear.

Chapter 14

The Basics

The Spanish Alphabet[1]

Letter	Pronunciation	Letter	Pronunciation
A	ah	O	oh
B	bay	P	pay
C	say	Q	koo
D	day	R	**ay**-ray
E	ay	RR	**ay**-rray OR **doh**-blay **ay**-ray
F	**ay**-fay	S	**ay**-say
G	hay	T	tay
H	**ah**-chay	U	oo
I	ee	V	bay OR **oo**-bay
J	**hoh**-tah	W	**doh**-blay bay OR **doh**-blay **oo**-bay
K	kah	X	**ay**-kees
L	**ay**-lay	Y	ee **gree**^**ay**-gah
M	**ay**-may	Z	**say**-tah
N	**ay**-nay	CH[2]	chay
Ñ	**ayn**-yay	LL[2]	**ay**-yay

Notes

[1] After practicing the alphabet, have students go to Chapter 18 and practice spelling the words aloud. Learning to spell in Spanish can be very useful, especially when helping a Spanish-speaker with names, addresses, etc. in English.

[2] These two sounds, once considered letters, no longer form part of the Spanish Alphabet. They have been included since they are commonly used in spelling.

Numbers[1]

Number	Pronunciation	Number	Pronunciation
0	**say**-roh	18	dee^ay-see-**oh**-choh
1	**oo**-noh	19	dee^ay-see-**noo^ay**-bay
2	dohs	20	**bayn**-tay
3	trays	21	**bayn**-tay ee **oo**-noh
4	**koo^ah**-troh	22	**bayn**-tay ee dohs
5	**seen**-koh	23	**bayn**-tay ee trays
6	say^ees	24	**bayn**-tay ee **koo^ah**-troh
7	**see^ay**-tay	25	**bayn**-tay ee **seen**-koh
8	**oh**-choh	26	**bayn**-tay ee say^ees
9	**noo^ay**-bay	27	**bayn**-tay ee **see^ay**-tay
10	**dee^ays**	28	**bayn**-tay ee **oh**-choh
11	**ohn**-say	29	**bayn**-tay ee **noo^ay**-bay
12	**doh**-say	30	**trayn**-tah
13	**tray**-say	31	**trayn**-tah ee **oo**-noh
14	kah-**tohr**-say	40	koo^ah-**rayn**-tah
15	**keen**-say	42	koo^ah-**rayn**-tah ee dohs
16	dee^ay-see-**say^ees**	50	seen-**koo^ayn**-tah
17	dee^ay-see-**see^ay**-tay	60	say-**sayn**-tah

Number	Pronunciation	Number	Pronunciation
70	say-**tayn**-tah	900	noh-bay-**see^ayn**-tohs
80	oh-**chayn**-tah	1.000	meel [2]
90	noh-**bayn**-tah	2.000	dohs meel
100	**see^ayn**	10.000	dee^ays meel
101	**see^ayn**-toh **oo**-noh	100.000	**see^ayn** meel
150	**see^ayn**-toh seen-**koo^ayn**-tah	200.000	dohs-**see^ayn**-tohs meel
200	doh-**see^ayn**-tohs	1.000.000	oon mee-**yohn**
300	tray-**see^ayn**-tohs	10.000.000	dee^ays mee-**yoh**-nays
400	koo^ah-troh-**see^ayn**-tohs	20.000.000	**bayn**-tay mee-**yoh**-nays
500	kee-**nee^ayn**-tohs	100.000.000	**see^ayn** mee-**yoh**-nays
600	say-**see^ayn**-tohs	200.000.000	dohs-**see^ayn**-tohs mee-**yoh**-nays
700	say-tay-**see^ayn**-tohs	1.000.000.000	meel mee-**yoh**-nays [3]
800	oh-choh-**see^ayn**-tohs	2.000.000.000	dohs meel mee-**yoh**-nays [3]

Notes

[1] The Spanish spellings have not been included since they are irrelevant for your purposes.

[2] Numbers in Spanish can become quite complicated. Therefore, when working with large sums, it is best to write them out and show the person. Also, remember, that when writing numbers in Spanish, commas become decimals and decimals become commas; this is the opposite of the English style of writing numbers.

[3] In American English, *1,000,000,000* would be expressed as *one billion* which is 10^9. However, in Spanish, this number would be written as *1.000.000.000* and would be expressed as *mil millones*, which literally means *one thousand millions*. The same is true of *2,000,000,000* and so on. The number for *one billion* in Spanish would actually be *1.000.000.000.000* which is 10^{12} and would be expressed as *un billón* which is *one trillion* in American English.

Chapter 15

Family and Friends

Before You Begin

The Hispanic culture places great emphasis on the family, both immediate and extended. Likewise, non-blood related friends may also be considered family and be treated the same. When seeking advice, great importance is placed on that received from family and friends alike rather than just one individual or institution. Therefore, the task of making an important decision will not necessarily be made only by the individual directly involved but rather through careful discussion with many of these persons mentioned. For example, you may hear a Hispanic reference the need to speak with his or her cousins *(primos [pree-mohs])* and automatically think they are blood relatives, when in fact, they may be just close family friends. You may need to ask to make sure that the person in question is truly a blood relative if this is a concern for you.

Phrases

English	Pronunciation & Spanish
1. He/She/This is my ...	*ays mee ...* Es mi ...
2. They/These are ...	*sohn mees ...* Son mis ...
3. mother	***mah**-dray* madre
4. father	***pah**-dray* padre
5. parents	***pah**-drays* padres
6. brother(s)	*ayr-**mah**-noh(s)* hermano(s) [1]
7. sister(s)	*ayr-**mah**-nah(s)* hermana(s) [1]
8. siblings [mixed group of boys and girls or all boys]	*ayr-**mah**-nohs* hermanos [1]
9. grandmother	*ah-**boo^ay**-lah* abuela

10. grandfather	*ah-**boo**^**ay**-loh* abuelo
11. grandparents	*ah-**boo**^**ay**-lohs* abuelos
12. son	***ee**-hoh* hijo
13. daughter	***ee**-hah* hija
14. children	***ee**-hohs* hijos
15. stepmother	*mah-**drah**-strah* madrastra
16. stepfather	*pah-**drah**-stroh* padrastro
17. stepbrother	*ayr-mah-**nah**-stroh* hermanastro
18. stepsister	*ayr-mah-**nah**-strah* hermanastra
19. stepchild	*ee-**hah**-stroh/strah* hijastro/a [2]
20. cousin	***pree**-moh/mah* primo/a [2]
21. aunt	***tee**-ah* tía
22. uncle	***tee**-oh* tío
23. nephew	*soh-**bree**-noh* sobrino
24. niece	*soh-**bree**-nah* sobrina
25. grandson	***nee**^**ay**-toh* nieto
26. granddaughter	***nee**^**ay**-tah* nieta
27. mother-in-law	***soo**^**ay**-grah* suegra
28. father-in-law	***soo**^**ay**-groh* suegro

29. brother-in-law	*koon-**yah**-doh* cuñado
30. sister-in-law	*koon-**yah**-dah* cuñada
31. son-in-law	***ee^ayr**-noh* yerno
32. daughter-in-law	***noo^ay**-rah* nuera
33. (legal) guardian	*too-**tohr** (lay-**gahl**)* tutor (legal)
34. godfather	*pah-**dree**-noh* padrino
35. godmother	*mah-**dree**-nah* madrina
36. godchild	*ah^ee-**hah**-doh/dah* ahijado/a [2]
37. sponsor	*pah-troh-see-nah-**dohr**(-ah)* patrocinador/a [2]
38. relatives	*pah-**ree^ayn**-tays* parientes
39. friend	*ah-**mee**-goh/gah* amigo/a [2]
40. boyfriend/fiancé	***noh**-bee^oh* novio
41. girlfriend/fiancée	***noh**-bee^ah* novia
42. budd(y/ies)/chum(s)	*kohm-**pah**-dray(s)* compadre(s)
43. close female friend(s)	*koh-**mah**-dray(s)* comadre(s)
44. Are you/Is he/she a blood relative?	*ays fah-mee-**lee^ahr** kohn-sahn-**ghee**-nay-oh?* ¿Es familiar consanguíneo?

Notes

[1] Use these three words as patterns for forming plural forms. Notice that in Spanish when referring to a group of people, one must take into account the number and gender of the persons he/she is addressing. If speaking to a group composed only of *males* or a group composed of *males* and *females* (regardless of how many men or women are present), the *–os* ending is used. When addressing a group of only *females*, the *–as* ending is used. You may want to ask your instructor for further clarification if you find this confusing.

[2] Use the *-o* ending for *males* and the *-a* ending for *females*.

Chapter 16

Expressing the Location of People, Places and Things

Phrases

English	Pronunciation & Spanish
1. Where is it/he/she?	*dohn-day ay-stah?* ¿Dónde está?
2. Where are they?	*dohn-day ay-stahn?* ¿Dónde están?
3. It/He/She is ...	*ay-stah ...* Está ...
4. They are ...	*ay-stahn ...* Están ...
5. here	*ah-kee* aquí
6. there	*ah-yee* allí
7. over there	*ah-yah* allá
8. up (there)	*(ah-yee) ah-rree-bah* (allí) arriba
9. down (there)	*(ah-yee) ah-bah-hoh* (allí) abajo
10. on top (of)	*ayn-see-mah (day)* encima (de)
11. below, underneath (something)	*day-bah-hoh (day)* debajo (de)
12. across (from) *or* facing	*ayn frayn-tay (day)* en frente (de)
13. behind (something)	*day-trahs (day)* detrás (de)
14. in front (of)	*day-lahn-tay (day)* delante (de)

15. close (to)	*sayr-kah (day)* **cerca (de)**
16. far (from)	*lay-hohs (day)* **lejos (de)**
17. at the bottom (of)	*ayn ayl fohn-doh (day)* **en el fondo (de)**
18. to the side (of)	*ahl lah-doh (day)* **al lado (de)**
19. to the right (of)	*ah lah day-ray-chah (day)* **a la derecha (de)**
20. to the left (of)	*ah lah ees-kee^ayr-dah (day)* **a la izquierda (de)**
21. in the middle (of)	*ayn ayl may-dee^oh (day)* **en el medio (de)**
22. between …	*ayn-tray* **entre …**
23. inside (of)	*(ah-)dayn-troh (day)* **(a)dentro (de)**
24. outside (of)	*(ah-)foo^ay-rah (day)* **(a)fuera (de)**
25. at home.	*ayn kah-sah.* **en casa.**
26. in the car / vehicle.	*ayn ayl kah-rroh / bay-ee-koo-loh.* **en el carro / vehículo.**
27. at my—'s house.	*ayn lah kah-sah day mee(s)—.* **en la casa de mi(s)—.** [1,2]
28. in my—'s car.	*ayn ayl kah-rroh day mee(s)—.* **en el carro de mi(s)—.** [1,2]
29. in …	*ayn …* **en …**
the cell.	*lah sayl-dah.* **la celda.**
the bag.	*lah bohl-sah.* **la bolsa.**
the pocket.	*ayl bohl-see-yoh.* **el bolsillo.**
the cabinet.	*ayl gah-bee-nay-tay.* **el gabinete.**
the glove compartment.	*lah goo^ahn-tay-rah.* **la guantera.**

the trunk [of a car].	*ayl mah-lay-**tay**-roh.* el maletero.
the trunk [for storage].	*ayl bah-**ool**.* el baúl.
the mattress.	*ayl kohl-**chohn**.* el colchón.
the drawer.	*lah gah-**bay**-tah.* la gaveta.

---

30. What is this?
*kay ays **ay**-stoh?*
¿Qué es esto? [3]

---

31. What is that?
*kay ays **ay**-soh?*
¿Qué es eso? [4]

---

32. What is that?
*kay ays ah-**kay**-yoh?*
¿Qué es aquello? [5]

Notes

[1] See *Chapter 15 - Family and Friends* for necessary vocabulary.

[2] You will hear *mi* in reference to a *singular* person or item and *mis* in reference is to a *plural* item or *two or more* people.

[3] Use *esto* when an item is in very close proximity, such as *"this here."*

[4] Use *eso* when an item is not nearby but not too far, such as *"that there."*

[5] Use *aquello* when an item is far or very far away, such as *"that over there."*

Practical Activities

A) Forming Detailed Questions with Location

Instructions: Review the possible translations for phrases 1 and 2 from this section. Notice that the concepts of *it* and *they* may be inferred. When wishing to add more detail to questions and expressions to avoid ambiguity, subjects can be added to these two questions. For example:

¿Dónde está? = Where is it/he/she? *compared to* ¿Dónde está + singular person/place/thing?
¿Dónde están? = Where are they? *compared to* ¿Dónde están + plural person/place/thing?

Practice combining these two questions according to the persons, places or things given below. Make sure to pay attention to singular and plural forms so as to match them with the appropriate questions. Feel free to consult the previous chapters if you need help with the Spanish pronunciation. Say each complete question aloud in Spanish then say the English translation. You may write these down for practice if you like.

1. the drugs/las drogas

2. the narcotics/los narcóticos

3. the weapon/el arma

4. the knife/el cuchillo

5. the gang members/los pandilleros

6. your husband/su esposo

7. your buddies/sus compadres

8. your stash/su escondite de drogas

B) Forming Detailed Statements and Responses with Location – Part 1

Instructions: Review the possible translations for phrases 3 and 4 from this section. Notice that the concepts of *it* and *they* may be inferred. When wishing to add more detail to a statement in order to avoid ambiguity, subjects can be added to these two phrases as well. For example:

Está ... = It/he/she is ... *compared to*   singular person/place/thing + está ...
Están ... = They are ... *compared to*   plural person/place/thing + están ...

Practice combining these two phrases according to the persons, places or things provided below. Make sure to pay attention to singular and plural forms so as to match them with the appropriate phrase. Feel free to consult the previous chapters if you need help with the Spanish pronunciation. Say each phrase aloud in Spanish then say the English translation. You may write these down for practice if you like. Notice these are not quite complete sentences ... yet!

1. the drugs/las drogas ...

2. the narcotics/los narcóticos ...

3. the weapon/el arma ...

4. the knife/el cuchillo ...

5. the gang members/los pandilleros ...

6. your husband/su esposo ...

7. your buddies/sus compadres ...

8. your stash/su escondite de drogas ...

C) Forming Detailed Statements and Responses with Location – Part 2

Instructions: In exercise B, you learned to form the beginning of what would become a very complete sentence, detailed, yet concise enough to provide you with necessary information. Now you will combine the beginning of each statement you formed from exercise B with its respective numbered ending provided below. For example:

The beginning of the sentence from number 1, exercise **B**, should read "*Las drogas están …*". Number 1, exercise **C**, reads "*allí abajo.*" Therefore, the entire statement would be "*Las drogas están allí abajo.*" – "*The drugs are there underneath.*"

1. down there/allí abajo

2. up here/aquí arriba

3. in the car/en el carro

4. in the mattress/en el colchón

5. in my brother's house/en la casa de mi hermano

6. at home/en casa

7. behind (over) there/allá detrás

8. in the trunk/en el baúl

Follow-up

Instructions: Now that you have successfully formed the eight questions and their eight complete answers, find a partner and designate one person as *el/la agente* and the other as *el/la sospechoso/a.* Have *el agente* ask the questions while *el sospechoso* must answer them. After you finish, switch roles and repeat the question/answer session again. Finally, try creating some of your own questions and answers. You may want to ask your instructor for assistance.

Chapter 17

Telling Time . . . The Easy Way

Phrases

English	Pronunciation & Spanish
1. It's (+ number) . . .	*ays lah (+ number) . . .* Es la (+ number) . . .[1] *sohn lahs (+ number) . . .* Son las (+ number) . . .[2]
2. . . . in the morning.	*. . . day lah mahn-**yah**-nah.* . . . de la mañana.[3]
3. . . . in the afternoon.	*. . . day lah **tahr**-day.* . . . de la tarde.[3]
4. . . . in the evening/at night.	*. . . day lah **noh**-chay.* . . . de la noche.[3]
5. At (+number) . . .	*ah lah (+ number) . . .* a la (+number) . . .[4] *ah lahs (+ number) . . .* a las (+number) . . .[5]
6. What time is it?	*kay **oh**-rah ays?* ¿Qué hora es?[6]
7. At what time is it?	*ah kay **oh**-rah ays?* ¿A qué hora es?[7]
8. It's midnight.	*ays lah may-dee^ah- **noh**-chay.* Es la medianoche.
9. It's noon.	*ays ayl may-dee^oh-**dee**-ah.* Es el mediodía.
10. At midnight.	*ah lah may-dee^ah-**noh**-chay.* A la medianoche.
11. At noon.	*ahl may-dee^oh -**dee**-ah.* Al mediodía.

12. Your appointment is . . .

*soo **see**-tah ays . . .*
Su cita es . . .

at one

*ah lah **oo**-nah*
a la una

at two

ah lahs dohs
a las dos

at three

ah lahs trays
a las tres

at four

*ah lahs **koo^ah**-troh*
a las cuatro

at five

*ah lahs **seen**-koh*
a las cinco

at six

ah lahs say^ees
a las seis

at seven

*ah lahs **see^ay**-tay*
a las siete

at eight

*ah lahs **oh**-choh*
a las ocho

at nine

*ah lahs **noo^ay**-bay*
a las nueve

at ten

ah lahs dee^ays
a las diez

at eleven

*ah lahs **ohn**-say*
a las once

at twelve

*ah lahs **doh**-say*
a las doce

fifteen

*ee **koo^ahr**-toh*
y cuarto

thirty

*ee **may**-dee^ah*
y media

forty-five

*ee koo^ah-**rayn**-tah ee **seen**-koh*
y cuarenta y cinco

in the morning.

*day lah mahn-**yay**-nah.*
de la mañana.

in the afternoon.

*day lah **tahr**-day.*
de la tarde.

in the evening.

*day lah **noh**-chay.*
de la noche.

Notes

[1] This phrase is used to answer the question *¿Qué hora es?* when the answer begins with *1 (pronounced **oo-nah**).*

[2] This phrase is used to answer the question *¿Qué hora es?* when the answer begins with *2 or more.*

[3] For simplicity's sake, use "*de la mañana*" from early morning (generally sun-up) to noon, "*de la tarde*" from noon to sun-down and "*de la noche*" from sun-down to early morning.

[4] This phrase is used to answer the question *¿A qué hora es?* when the answer begins with *1 (pronounced **oo-nah**).*

[5] This phrase is used to answer the question *¿A qué hora es?* when the answer begins with *2 or more.*

[6] Use this question for asking the time in general.

[7] Use this question for asking at what time an event is or starts.

Practical Activities

A) Telling time

Instructions: Draw the hands on the blank clock faces according to the SPANISH phrase given below each one. Then, label the hands with the appropriate number. Lastly, write A.M. or P.M. in the upper right-hand corner of each square indicating the time of day of the appointment. Only look back at the phrases in the chapter after you have finished to check your answers.

Su cita es . . .

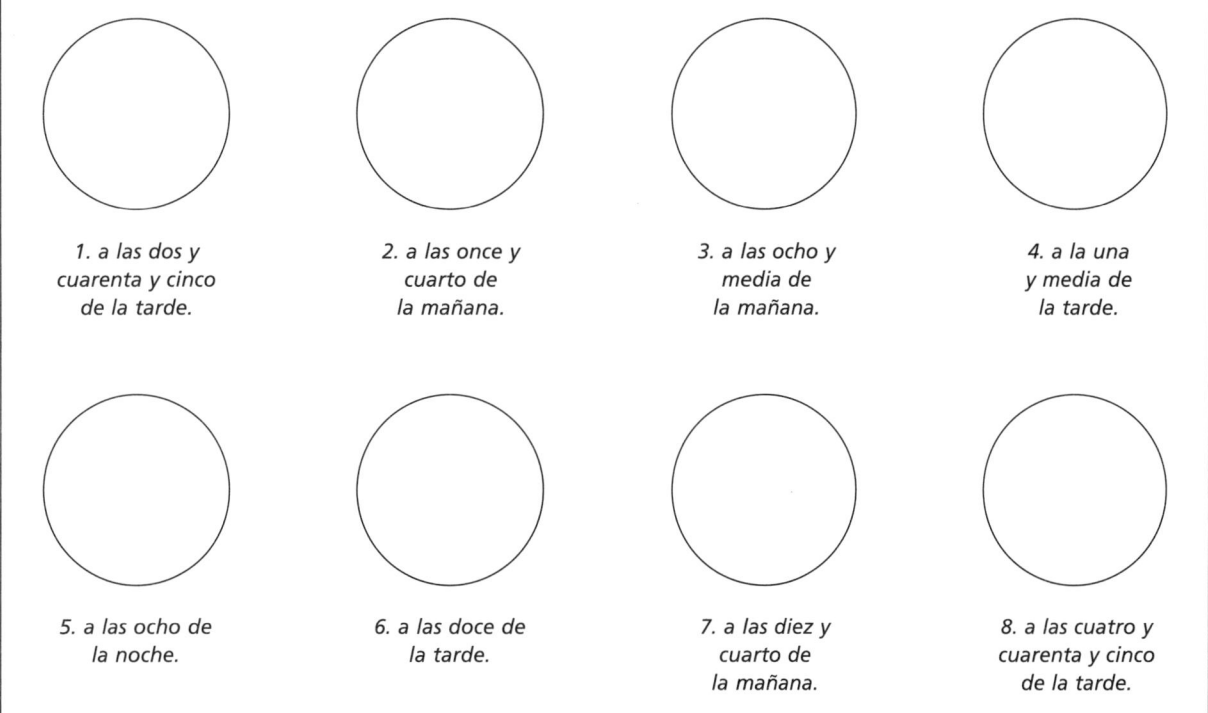

1. a las dos y cuarenta y cinco de la tarde.

2. a las once y cuarto de la mañana.

3. a las ocho y media de la mañana.

4. a la una y media de la tarde.

5. a las ocho de la noche.

6. a las doce de la tarde.

7. a las diez y cuarto de la mañana.

8. a las cuatro y cuarenta y cinco de la tarde.

B) Oral Practice

Instructions: Practice saying the appointment time aloud in Spanish for each clock face given in exercise **A**. Then change the structure of the sentence to simply state the time and practice those phrases aloud. Review **NOTES 6** and **7** from this section for more explanation.

For example:

Su cita es a las doce y cuarto de la tarde. – This phrase specifies the time of an event.
(Your appointment is at 12:15 in the afternoon.)

Change it to read:

Son las doce y cuarto de la tarde. – Now, this phrase merely states the time.
(It's 12:15 in the afternoon.)

Days, Months and Dates[1]

Phrases

English	Pronunciation & Spanish
1. Monday	*loo*-nays lunes
2. Tuesday	*mahr*-tays martes
3. Wednesday	mee-*ayr*-koh-lays miércoles
4. Thursday	*hoo^ay*-bays jueves
5. Friday	*bee^ayr*-nays viernes
6. Saturday	*sah*-bah-doh sábado
7. Sunday	doh-*meen*-goh domingo
8. January	ay-*nay*-roh enero
9. February	fay-*bray*-roh febrero
10. March	*mahr*-soh marzo
11. April	ah-*breel* abril
12. May	*mah*-yoh mayo
13. June	*hoo*-nee^oh junio
14. July	*hoo*-lee^oh julio
15. August	ah-*goh*-stoh agosto
16. September	sayp-*tee^aym*-bray septiembre
17. October	ohk-*too*-bray octubre

18. November	*noh-**bee^aym**-bray* noviembre
19. December	*dee-**see^aym**-bray* diciembre
20. The (#) of (month) of (year).	*ayl — day — day —.* El — de — de —. [2]
21. The first of (month).	*ayl pree-**may**-roh day —.* El primero de —.

Notes

[1] Unlike English, days of the week and months of the year should never be capitalized. However, capitalization of these words in Spanish is often seen in journalistic style writing.

[2] Reference *Chapter 14 – The Basics – Numbers* to assist you with dates. Make sure to review **Before You Begin** from *Chapter 5 – Parole and Probation Specifics – Identifying Clients and Confirming Appointments* for an explanation of how written dates may differ from Spanish to English.

Chapter 18

Parts of the Body

Phrases:

English	Pronunciation & Spanish
the human body	*ayl koo^ayr-poh oo-mah-noh* el cuerpo humano
head	*lah kah-bay-sah* la cabeza
neck	*ayl koo^ay-yoh* el cuello
chest	*ayl pay-choh* el pecho
breast	*ayl say-noh* el seno
nipple	*ayl pay-sohn* el pezón
rib	*lah koh-stee-yah* la costilla
stomach	*ayl ay-stoh-mah-goh* el estómago
navel	*ayl ohm-blee-goh* el ombligo
thigh	*ayl moo-sloh* el muslo
knee	*lah rroh-dee-yah* la rodilla
calf	*lah pahn-toh-ree-yah* la pantorilla
shin	*lah ay-spee-nee-yah* la espinilla
ankle	*ayl toh-bee-yoh* el tobillo

foot	*ayl pee^ay* **el pie**
toe	*ayl **day**-doh (dayl pee^ay)* **el dedo (del pie)**
finger	*ayl **day**-doh* **el dedo**
nail	*lah **oon**-yah* **la uña**
chin	*lah bahr-**bee**-yah* **la barbilla**
hand	*lah **mah**-noh* **la mano**
wrist	*lah moon-**yay**-kah* **la muñeca**
abdomen	*ayl ahb-**doh**-mayn* **el abdomen**
arm	*ayl **brah**-soh* **el brazo**
elbow	*ayl **koh**-doh* **el codo**
face	*lah **kah**-rah* **la cara**
eye	*ayl **oh**-hoh* **el ojo**
nose	*lah nah-**rees*** **la nariz**
mouth	*lah **boh**-kah* **la boca**
lip	*ayl **lah**-bee^oh* **el labio**
cheek	*lah may-**hee**-yah* **la mejilla**
forehead	*lah **frayn**-tay* **la frente**
eye lid	*ayl **pahr**-pah-doh* **el párpado**
inner ear	*ayl oh-**ee**-doh* **el oído**
outer ear	*lah oh-**ray**-hah* **la oreja**

shoulder	*ayl **ohm**-broh* el hombro
back	*lah ay-**spahl**-dah* la espalda
waist	*lah seen-**too**-rah* la cintura
hip	*lah kah-**day**-rah* la cadera
buttock	*lah **nahl**-gah* la nalga [1]
leg	*lah **pee^ayr**-nah* la pierna
heel	*ayl tah-**lohn*** el talón
coccyx	*ayl **kohk**-seeks* el cóccix [2]
nape	*lah **noo**-kah* la nuca
hamstring	*ayl poh-stay-**ree^ohr** dayl **moo**-sloh* el posterior del muslo
palm	*lah **pahl**-mah* la palma
thorax	*ayl **toh**-rahks* el tórax
groin	*lah **een**-glay* la ingle
forearm	*ayl ahn-tay-**brah**-soh* el antebrazo
armpit	*lah ahk-**see**-lah* la axila [3]
eyebrow	*lah **say**-hah* la ceja
temple	*lah see^ayn* la sien

NOTES:

[1] The plural form of la nalga, which is las nalgas, may be considered rude by some Hispanics. However, las asentaderas (lahs ah-sayn-tah-**day**-rahs) is a non-offensive, lower-register term that may be used.

[2] Another common term for cóccix is la rabadilla (lah rrah-bah-**dee**-yah).

[3] Another common term for axila is el sobaco (ayl soh-**bah**-koh) but is a lower register.

The Organs

Phrases:

English	Pronunciation & Spanish
internal organs	*lohs **ohr**-gah-nohs een-**tayr**-nohs* los órganos internos
brain	*ayl say-**ray**-broh* el cerebro
spinal cord	*lah **may**-doo-lah ay-spee-**nahl*** la médula espinal
tongue	*lah **layn**-goo^ah* la lengua
liver	*ayl **ee**-gah-doh* el hígado
esophagus	*ayl ay-**soh**-fah-goh* el esófago
pancreas	*ayl **pahn**-kray-ahs* el páncreas
diaphragm	*ayl dee^ah-**frahg**-mah* el diafragma
spleen	*ayl **bah**-soh* el bazo
lungs	*lohs pool-**moh**-nays* los pulmones
heart	*ayl koh-rah-**sohn*** el corazón
stomach	*ayl ay-**stoh**-mah-goh* el estómago
gallbladder	*lah bay-**see**-koo-lah bee-**lee**^ahr* la vesícula biliar
kidneys	*lohs rreen-**yoh**-nays* los riñones
digestive system	*ayl see-**stay**-mah dee-hay-**stee**-boh* el sistema digestivo
small intestine	*ayl een-tay-**stee**-noh dayl-**gah**-doh* el intestino delgado
large intestine	*ayl een-tay-**stee**-noh **groo**^ay-soh* el intestino grueso

rectum	*ayl **rrayk**-toh* el recto
appendix	*ayl ah-**payn**-dee-say* el apéndice
anus	*ayl **ah**-noh* el ano
reproductive organs	*lohs **ohr**-gah-nohs rray-proh-dook-**tee**-bohs* los órganos reproductivos
fallopian tubes	*lahs **trohm**-pahs* las trompas
ovaries	*lohs oh-**bah**-ree^ohs* los ovarios
uterus	*ayl **oo**-tay-roh* el útero [1]
cervix	*ayl **koo^ay**-yoh dayl **oo**-tay-roh* el cuello del útero
vagina	*lah bah-**hee**-nah* la vagina
seminal vesicle	*ayl bay-**see**-koo-loh say-mee-**nahl*** el vesículo seminal
prostate gland	*lah **proh**-stah-tah* la próstata
urethra	*lah oo-**ray**-trah* la uretra
testicles	*lohs tay-**stee**-koo-lohs* los testículos
scrotum	*ayl ay-**skroh**-toh* el escroto
penis	*ayl **pay**-nay* el pene
prepuce, foreskin	*ayl pray-**poo**-see^oh* el prepucio
vas deferens	*lohs kohn-**dook**-tohs day-fay-**rayn**-tays* los conductos deferentes
bladder	*lah bay-**hee**-gah* la vejiga

NOTES:

[1] Another term for el útero is la matriz (lah mah-**trees**).

Appendix

Metric Conversion Quick Reference

Quick Reference Height Chart

Feet / Inches	Centimeters	Feet/Inches	Centimeters
4'5"	135 cm	5'8"	173 cm
4'6"	137 cm	5'9"	175 cm
4'7"	140 cm	5'10"	178 cm
4'8"	142 cm	5'11"	180 cm
4'9"	145 cm	6'	183 cm
4'10"	147 cm	6'1"	185 cm
4'11"	150 cm	6'2"	188 cm
5'	152 cm	6'3"	191 cm
5'1"	155 cm	6'4"	193 cm
5'2"	157 cm	6'5"	196 cm
5'3"	160 cm	6'6"	198 cm
5'4"	163 cm	6'7"	201 cm
5'5"	165 cm	6'8"	203 cm
5'6"	168 cm	6'9"	206 cm
5'7"	170 cm	6'10"	208 cm

Length/Speed

1 inch = 2.540 centimeters
1 centimeter = 0.3937 inches
1 foot = 30.48 centimeters
1 mile = 1.609 kilometers
1 kilometer = 0.6214 miles

examples:
8 inches × 2.540 centimeters = 20.32 centimeters
36 centimeters × 0.3937 inches = 14.1732 inches
3 feet × 30.48 centimeters = 91.44 centimeters
15 miles × 1.609 kilometers = 24.135 kilometers
30 kilometers × 0.6214 miles = 18.6411 miles

Weight

1 Pound = .453 Kilogram
1 Kilogram = 2.2 pounds

examples:
115 pounds × .453 kilogram = 52.095 kilograms
75 kilograms × 2.2 pounds = 165 pounds

For online tables, charts and converters, also see one of these helpful free sites:*
http://www.sciencemadesimple.com/conversions.html
http://www.albireo.ch/bodyconverter/
http://www.teaching-english-in-japan.net/conversion/

  *These sites are not affiliated with this text in any way.

Nationalities/Countries[1]

Country	Nationality
pah-ees país	*nah-see^oh-nah-lee-dahd* nacionalidad
Argentina *ahr-hayn-tee-nah* Argentina	Argentine *ahr-hayn-tee-noh/nah* argentino/a
Bolivia *boh-lee-bee^ah* Bolivia	Bolivian *boh-lee-bee^ah-noh/nah* boliviano/a
Chile *chee-lay* Chile	Chilean *chee-lay-noh/nah* chileno/a
Columbia *koh-lohm-bee^ah* Colombia	Columbian *koh-lohm-bee^ah-noh/nah* colombiano/a
Costa Rica *koh-stah rree-kah* Costa Rica	Costa Rican *koh-stah-rree-sayn-say* costarricense
Cuba *koo-bah* Cuba	Cuban *koo-bah-noh/nah* cubano/a
Dominican Republic *lah rray-poo-blee-kah doh-mee-nee-kah-nah* La República Dominicana	Dominican *doh-mee-nee-kah-noh/nah* dominicano/a

Ecuador	Ecuadorean
*ay-koo^ah-**dohr***	*ay-koo^ah-toh-**ree^ah**-noh/nah*
Ecuador	ecuatoriano/a
El Salvador	Salvadoran
*ayl sahl-bah-**dohr***	*sahl-bah-doh-**rayn**-yoh/yah*
El Salvador	salvadoreño/a
Guatemala	Guatemalan
*goo^ah-tah-**mah**-lah*	*goo^ah-tay-mahl-**tay**-koh/kah*
Guatemala	guatemalteco/a
Honduras	Honduran
*ohn-**doo**-rahs*	*ohn-doo-**rayn**-yoh/yah*
Honduras	hondureño/a
Nicaragua	Nicaraguan
*nee-kah-**rah**-goo^ah*	*nee-kah-rah-**goo^ayn**-say*
Nicaragua	nicaragüense
Panama	Panamanian
*pah-nah-**mah***	*pah-nah-**mayn**-yoh/yah*
Panamá	panameño/a
Paraguay	Paraguayan
*pah-rah-**gwah^ee***	*pah-rah-**gwah^ee**-yoh-yah*
Paraguay	paraguayo/a
Peru	Peruvean
*pay-**roo***	*pay-**roo^ah**-noh/nah*
Perú	peruano/a
Puerto Rico	Puerto Rican
***poo^ayr**-toh **rree**-koh*	*poo^ayr-toh-rree-**kayn**-yoh/yah*
Puerto Rico	puertorriqueño/a
Spain	Spanish
*ay-**spahn**-yah*	*ay-spahn-**yohl**(-lah)*
España	español/a²
United States	American
*ay-**stah**-dohs oo-**nee**-dohs*	*ay-stah-doh-oo-nee-**dayn**-say*
Estados Unidos	estadounidense
Uruguay	Uruguayan
*oo-roo-**gwah^ee***	*oo-roo-**gwah^ee**-yoh/yah*
Uruguay	uruguayo/a
Venezuela	Venezuelan
*bay-nay-**soo^ay**-lah*	*bayn-nay-soh-**lah**-noh/nah*
Venezuela	venezolano/a

Notes

[1] You will hear a *male* use the *–o ending* and a *female* use the *–a ending* where indicated. Otherwise, when no option is given, this indicates that the same word may be used to refer to a *male* or a *female*. For example, *costarricense* allows for no gender distinction.

[2] Notice with this word, the form referring to a *male* ends in *–l*; the *–a ending* is added to this to create the form referring to a *female*.

Major Religious Affiliations[1]

Catholic	kah-**toh**-lee-koh/kah católico/a
Protestant	proh-tay-**stahn**-tay protestante
Baptist	bah^oo-**tee**-stah bautista
Jehovah's Witness	tay-**stee**-goh/gah day hay-oh-**bah** testigo/a de Jehová
Methodist	may-toh-**dee**-stah metodista
Lutheran	loo-tay-**rahn**-noh/nah luterano/a
Presbyterian	prays-bee-tay-**ree^ah**-noh/nah presbiteriano
Mormon	mohr-**mohn**(-ah) mormón/a [2]
Seventh Day Adventist	ahd-bahn-**tee**-stah adventista
Jewish	hoo-**dee**-oh/ah judío/a
Buddist	boo-**dee**-stah budista
Muslim	moo-sool-**mahn**(-ah) musulmán/a [2]
atheist	ah-**tey**-oh/ah ateo/a
agnostic	ahg-**noh**-stee-koh/kah agnóstico/a
Christian Science	kree-**stee^ah**-noh/nah see^ayn-**tee**-fee-koh/kah cristiano/a científico/a [1]

Notes

[1] You will hear a *male* use the *–o ending* and a *female* use the *–a ending* where indicated. Otherwise, when no option is given, this indicates that the same word may be used to refer to a *male* or a *female*. For example, *bud-ista* allows for no gender distinction.

[2] Notice with this word, the form referring to a *male* ends in *–m*; the *–a ending* is added to this to create the form which refers to a *female*.

Bibliography

About: Mathematics. Deb Russell. 2007. 21 Sept. 2007 http://math.about.com/library/weekly/aa070502a.htm.

About: Spanish Language. Gerald Erichsen. 2007. 15 Aug. 2007 http://spanish.about.com/od/wordlists/a/clothing.htm.

"Aging Gracefully, Live Longer, Liver Better." *American Family.* Public Broadcasting Service. 2004. 8 Aug. 2007 http://www.pbs.org/americanfamily/aging.html.

Alcohol en la comunidad hispana. Recovery Month. 4 April 2007 http://www.recoverymonth.gov/2007/multimedia/w.aspx?ID=490.

Alonso, Alex. *Street Gangs.* http://www.streetgangs.com/.

American Civil Liberties Union. "La lucha contra los abusos de la policía: Manual de acción comunitaria." *Departamento de Educación Pública de la ACLU.* Ed. Rozella Kennedy. 1998. 17 April 2007 www.peoples-law.org/multilingual/spanish/s-police_abuse.pdf.

"Caló." *Wikipedia.* 1 July 2007 http://en.wikipedia.org/wiki/Cal%C3%B3_(Chicano).

Cloud Jr., Sanford. "Taking America's Pulse: A Nationwide Survey Shows Prejudice and Discrimination Against Minority Americans Continue but Finds Encouraging Trends." *Focus.* 29:5 2001. 25 April 2007 http://www.jointcenter.org/publications1/focus/focusPDFs/2001/may01.pdf.

Collin, P. H. and Lourdes Melcion. *Spanish Law Dictionary.* Great Britain: Peter Collin Publishing, 1999.

Cuevas de Cassie, Rebecca M. "Hispanic Values Tradition." *BellaOnline The Voice of Women* (2007): 9 Sept. 2007 http://www.bellaonline.com/articles/art28296.asp.

Cuevas de Cassie, Rebecca M. "Hispanic Values Respect." *BellaOnline The Voice of Women* (2007): 9 Sept. 2007 http://www.bellaonline.com/articles/art31981.asp.

Diccionario de Reggaeton. Ed. Daniel Santiago. 2007 http://www.mundoreggaeton.com/diccionario/.

Double-Tongued Dictionary. Ed. Grant Barrett. Electronic Ed., 2007 http://doubletongued.org/index.php/dictionary/guide/.

Erker, et. al. "Field Sobriety Test." *EN&H Law.* 2007 http://www.enhlaw.com/ks_dui_field_test.htm.

Farrar, Johnathan D. "Transparency and the Rule of Law in Latin America." *U.S. Department of State.* 25 May 2005. 20 June 2007 http://www.state.gov/p/inl/rls/rm/46913.htm.

"Field Sobriety Evaluations or 'Tests." *DrunkDrivingDefense.com.* 2007 http://www.drunkdrivingdefense.com/general/field-sobriety-evaluations-or-tests.htm.

Gaviria, Alejandro and Carmen Pagés. "Patterns of Crime Victimization in Latin America." *Inter-American Development Bank.* Washington, DC: Inter-American Development Bank. 29 Oct. 1999. 15 June 2007 http://www.iadb.org/res/publications/pubfiles/pubWP-408.pdf..

"Gang Slang." *Gangs.* 2007 http://www.angelfire.com/ga3/latingangs/123.html.

Harvey, William C. *Spanish for Law Enforcement Personnel.* Hauppauge, New York: Barron's, 1996.

Hernández, et. al. *Jergas de habla hispana.* 3 Nov. 2007 http://www.jergasdehablahispana.org/index.php?pais=M%E9xico&palabra=jefe&tipobusqueda=1.

Johnson, Stephen. "Latin America." *The Heritage Foundation.* 2006. 2 Aug. 2007 http://www.heritage.org/Research/features/issues/issuearea/LatinAmerica.cfm.

Kaplan, Steven M. *English-Spanish Spanish-English Legal Dictionary.* 2nd ed. New York: Aspen, 2001.

Labredo, Ana C. Jarvis. *Spanish for Law Enforcement.* Boston: Houghton Mifflin, 2000.

Leet, Rush, and Anthony M. Smith. *Gangs, Graffiti and Violence: A Realistic Guide to the Scope and Nature of Gangs in America.* Incline Village, Nevada: Copperhouse, 2000.

Lewis, Jared. *Know Gangs*. http://www.knowgangs.com/.

Little, Ken. "Hispanics in crashes lead DWI stats." *StarNewsOnline*. 22 June 2006. 17 July 2007
    http://www.starnewsonline.com/apps/pbcs.dll/article?AID=/20060622/NEWS/606220415/1004.

Los hispanos y la violencia con las armas de fuego. Violence Policy Center. 8 May 2001 http://www.vpc.org/
    studies/espexec.htm.

"Mexican Gangs." *Criminal Street Gang Intelligence*. 2 Oct. 2007 http://www.nationalconcernedofficers.com/
    Mexican%20Gangs.htm.

Mikkelson, Holly. *The Interpreter's Companion*. 4th ed. USA: Acebo, 2000.

Murray, Bridget. "Cultural insensitivity leads to unfair penalties." *APA Monitor Online*. 30.9 (1999). 26 July
    2007 http://www.apa.org/monitor/oct99/mv2.html.

National Highway Safetly Traffic Administration. "Lives Still at Risk: A Look at the Groups that Traffic Safety
    Has Left Behind." *Traffic Safety Center Online Newsletter*. 1:4 2003. 5 May 2007.
    http://www.tsc.berkeley.edu/newsletter/Fall03/left_behind.html.

New Century Foundation. *The Color of Crime: Race, Crime and Violence in America*. 2005
    www.amren.com/colorofcrime/color.pdf

Puentes, Yvonne. "Ethnic Terms Can Cause Confusion." *Borderlands* 17 (1998-1999): 16.

Robles-Peña, Angel R.."Reforma migratoria: La ley Strive." *MSNLatino Noticias: Inmigración*.
    http://latino.msn.com/noticias/inmigracion/articlepage.aspx?cp-documentid=4750808.

SC.GOV. "Public Safety Issues." The Official Website for the State of South Carolina. 2005. 5 April 2007
    http://www.state.sc.us/cma/Hispanic_Report/htm/Public_Safety.htm.

Serano, Julian. "Borderline definitions sink the debate." *The News & Observer* 30 June 2007
    http://www.newsobserver.com/print/saturday/opinion/story/622015.html.

"A Summary of the Proceedings." *Hispanic Outreach Forum and Law Enforcement Workshop*. Federal Trade
    Commission. Oct. 2004. http://www.nlpoa.org/FTC_Hispanic_Outreach_forum_and_Law_
    Enforcement_October_2004_NLPOA.pdf.

Terry-Azíos, Diana. "The State of Hispanic Health." *Latina Style* May/June 2007. 18 July 2007
    http://www.latinastyle.com/currentissue/v11-3/f-hispanichealth.html.

To Ask or Not to Ask? The Gilroy Dispatch. 5 July 2007. 10 Sept. 2007
    http://gilroydispatch.com/news/contentview.asp?c=218741.

Urban Dictionary. Ed. Aaron Peckham. Electronic Ed., 2007 http://www.urbandictionary.com/.

U.S. Department of Health and Human Services. "A Toolkit for Hispanic/Latino Community Groups." *Alcohol
    & Drug Information*. 20 Aug. 2007 http://ncadi.samhsa.gov/initiatives/hisplatino/community/
    toolkiteng.aspx.

U.S. Department of State's Bureau of International Information Programs. "Crime Hinders Development,
    Democracry in Latin America, U.S. Says." *International Information Programs*. 20 April 2005. 12 April
    2007 http://usinfo.state.gov/xarchives/display.html?p=washfile-english&y=2005&m=April&x=
    20050420161901ASrelliM0.5433161.

Weich, Ronald and Carlos Angulo. "Racial Disparities in the American Criminal Justice System." *Citizens
    Commission on Civil Rights*. 185-217. http://www.cccr.org/chapter14.pdf.

Williamson, David. "UNC, Wake Forest scholars work to reduce crimes against Hispanics in North Carolina."
    EurekAlert. 21 Feb. 2002. 5 March 2007 http://www.eurekalert.org/pub_releases/2002-02/
    uonc-uwf021802.php.

Zalaquett, Carlos. "His/Her Name is Today: Teaching." http://www.coedu.usf.edu/zalaquett/hoy/teaching.html.